# TAX THE RICH!

## How Lies, Loopholes, and Lobbyists
## Make the Rich Even Richer

By Morris Pearl, Erica Payne,
and the Patriotic Millionaires

D0188114

THE
NEW
PRESS

NEW YORK
LONDON

© 2021 for the compilation by The Patriotic Millionaires
All rights reserved.
No part of this book may be reproduced, in any form, without written permission from the publisher.

Requests for permission to reproduce selections from this book should be made through our website: thenewpress.com/contact.

Published in the United States by The New Press, New York, 2021
Distributed by Two Rivers Distribution

ISBN 978-1-62097-626-5 (pb)
ISBN 978-1-62097-664-7 (ebook)
CIP data is available

The New Press publishes books that promote and enrich public discussion and understanding of the issues vital to our democracy and to a more equitable world. These books are made possible by the enthusiasm of our readers; the support of a committed group of donors, large and small; the collaboration of our many partners in the independent media and the not-for-profit sector; booksellers, who often hand-sell New Press books; librarians; and above all by our authors.

www.thenewpress.com

*Book design and composition by Bookbright Media*
*This book was set in Minion and Interval Next*

Printed in the United States of America

10 9 8 7 6 5 4 3 2 1

# TAX THE RICH!

**Also by Morris Pearl**

*How to Think like a Patriotic Millionaire: Taxes*

**Also by Erica Payne**

*The Practical Progressive: How to Build a Twenty-First-Century Political Movement*

# Contents

# A Note from Morris Pearl

Dear Reader,

An article in the *New Yorker* a while back described a bunch of millionaires and billionaires building luxury bomb shelters on private islands in anticipation of some sort of apocalyptic scenario—high-end sanctuaries for the end of days. It made me angry and kind of sad too. These people are willing to pay millions to live through the collapse of society in comfort, but how many of them have spent millions—or any amount, for that matter—to change the dynamics that caused the threat in the first place? How many of those millionaires are willing to admit that they helped create or worsen the societal conditions that are causing their fear? Do any of them understand that much of—even most of—what is happening today is their fault?

A single day's worth of headlines can be enough to give even the most optimistic person doubt that we can find our way forward. All is not lost, but we do have some serious work to do. And it's abundantly clear that it's going to be much, much harder to do that work if my fellow millionaires and billionaires don't become part of the solution, or at least stop making all the problems we have worse.

I wrote this book in part to challenge my fellow millionaires to get their heads out of the sand. You are destroying the country, our country, my country. All of us, including us rich people, are going to end up paying the price unless we change course. Now.

I've got a message—a warning, really—for my fellow rich people, both in the United States and around the world. You cannot continue to sit by and enjoy your riches while the rest of the world falls further into poverty and chaos. We have seen the results of gross inequality over and over again. Reread your history books. Dysfunctional societies don't end well for rich people either.

I remember thinking about this years ago when I saw *Les Misérables* and heard the lines:

> *With all the anger in the land*
> *How long before the judgment day?*
> *Before we cut the fat ones down to size?*
> *Before the barricades arise?*

The play is set in Paris in the 1830s during what was known as the Second French Revolution, but it could have been set in Russia in 1917 or South Africa in the 1980s. Or America today.

History is riddled with examples of what happens when too many have too little and too few have too much. I'm not talking about a stock-market crash; I'm talking about a revolution. America's millionaires should know that during the 2016 election, 81% of Trump supporters and 79% of Bernie Sanders supporters said the country needed a political revolution.[1] Righteous anger is clearly not partisan.

Nick Hanauer, another millionaire deeply concerned about the state of things, sounded the alarm in a Politico piece titled

Peasants burning royal carriages during the French Revolution.

"The Pitchforks Are Coming . . . For Us Plutocrats." He got it mostly right. But it won't be pitchforks. U.S. civilians own more than 393 million guns, 120 guns for every one hundred residents.[2]

I want to ask my fellow millionaires, Do you really think you can protect yourself from mobs of angry, hungry people? So did King Louis XVI and Czar Nicholas II. You may believe that this time it will be different. You may think that your fancy little bunker will protect you. And perhaps you will be proven right. But I wouldn't count on the walls holding the world out forever, particularly when you live in a country with more guns than people.

To be clear, I don't feel guilty about being rich. I like being rich. I would recommend it to anyone. And I don't consider myself any more altruistic than the next person. I'm just as greedy as every other rich person I know. I'm just greedy for a different kind of country than a lot of other rich people are.

I'm greedy for a country with a basic sense of fairness for my family and me to live in. I'm greedy for a country where good businesses thrive and hard work is valued and fairly compensated. Where people feel safe in their neighborhoods. Where parents can tell their children that they're going to be okay and really believe it. I want to live in a country with lots of rich people and a huge middle class, and I happen to believe that lessening inequality by taxing rich people is the only way to create that kind of country.

Taxing our richest citizens is not the only thing we have to do, of course, but it is *not optional*. Think of it as entirely necessary, if not entirely sufficient. So I plan to do everything

"How do you feel about staying in power?"

I can to ensure we tax people like me as substantially and effectively as possible. Because I don't want to be a rich man in a poor country. It's just that simple. I don't want to live in a country with a few extraordinarily wealthy people and millions of poor people. And before you ask, no, I don't want to live there even if I happen to be one of the very rich people. I don't want to live behind barbed-wire fences. I don't want to ride around town in a bulletproof car with a trained security guard. I don't want to worry that my children or grandchildren are going to get kidnapped, or worse.

My daughter-in-law is Peruvian, and since she and my son met, my family and I have spent a lot of time in Peru. It's beautiful, but it's also profoundly disturbing to see its people struggle through deep, desperate poverty while the elites huddle with their wealth behind barbed-wire fences. I don't want to live in a country like that, but that's where we're heading.

There's a Greek proverb that goes, "A society grows great when old men plant trees whose shade they know they will never sit in." Lately, the old men running our country haven't been planting trees; they've been cutting them down to make room for private golf courses. And, yes, sadly, it is still mostly men.

We can fix the problem, or at least get a really good start on fixing it, relatively easily. It will take some time and money, but the solutions are fairly straightforward. And I, personally, would rather fix things than retreat into a gated community with a private security force while the world outside the gates falls apart.

## The Patriotic Millionaires

Luckily, I'm not alone. Ten years ago, with a few dozen other millionaires, I signed an open letter to America's leaders to protest the extension of the Bush tax cuts for people like us with incomes of over $1 million a year and/or assets of at least $5 million. Since then, this group of "Patriotic Millionaires" has grown to over two hundred people from thirty-three states. Now, keep in mind, there are about 500,000 people in the United States who make more than a million dollars a year, so we have some work to do on our recruiting, but it's a start.

At the time we released our initial letter, the disparity between the rich and the poor in America was the highest it had been in a hundred years, and it had reached a point that history proved was really problematic. It's only gotten worse since, with inequality continuing to rise even faster, destabilizing our society and eroding the foundation that had kept us strong for so long. We decided to focus our attention there, on the cancerous inequality at the center of our shared experience. It made sense, really, because we have been the beneficiaries of the economic system that created the disparity, and we have a personal understanding of its inner workings.

The tax system was our first target. But we expanded our fight beyond tax policy to include two other areas we think are essential for our long-term stability and prosperity: first, a top-to-bottom reform of our political system to limit the power of millionaires in our lawmaking (starting with taking a hatchet to our corrupt campaign-finance system),

Patriotic Millionaires stand with President Barack Obama for Tax Day Address,
April 11, 2012.

and, second, a reset of our wage and labor laws to ensure that working people, including those in the new "gig" economy, are guaranteed a fair share of the proceeds of business and paid a wage they can actually survive on.

If we achieve all our goals—higher taxes on millionaires, equal political representation for all Americans, and a living wage for working people—we will become a more equal and more stable nation over time. And, yes, a more prosperous nation overall as well (albeit one with slightly less-prosperous billionaires). I look forward to being a rich man in a rich, stable country.

Of course, there are still quite a few things standing in our way, not least among them several thousand millionaires who totally disagree with us. But we know the game—the lobbyists, the loopholes, and the lies. We know that public speeches about reform cover up special deals for rich donors on both sides of the political aisle. We know that if you look closely at the tax code, you will see nothing but layers upon layers of corruption and campaign contributions. We are insiders, with all the knowledge and access and power that comes with being rich in America. We have a unique ability, and a profound responsibility, to expose the lies, strip out what's broken, and create a tax system that ensures the economy works for everyone (including, by the way, rich folks).

Before I really got into political activism, I had a long career on Wall Street, capped off with a job at BlackRock, the world's largest asset-management firm. I remember having lunch one day during a break from a due-diligence meeting in the penthouse conference room of a bank headquarters in Athens, Greece. I picked up some dessert from a buffet and walked over to the window (so people wouldn't see that I was having two chocolate puddings). I looked out the window and thought I was seeing a parade, and I was thinking that was odd because it wasn't a holiday. And then I realized that I was watching a protest going toward Syntagma Square and the Greek parliament.

I watched the procession for a minute while finishing my pudding, and as I turned around to walk back to the table, I wondered if I was doing any good for any of the people of Greece besides the bankers I was having lunch with. There are few moments of perfect clarity in life; that was one of mine. Shortly afterward, I decided that I had done as much as I could for the shareholders of BlackRock. I quit my job and joined the Patriotic Millionaires as chair of the board and a full-time volunteer.

I now work full-time on policy and politics and have seen up-close how the whole political and legislative process works. They call it "sausage making" for a reason, and I can certainly understand why this messy process doesn't engender a lot of confidence. But the policy decisions our elected officials make affect people's lives in enormous ways. As citizens, we have a responsibility to understand that and try to avoid approaching politics as a spectator sport, cheering on our respective teams with no regard for the actual policy choices they make. Tax policy in particular deserves special attention because even small changes to it can have enormous implications for the well-being of our people.

I don't know if any two people can ever be completely in sync—and a couple hundred millionaires are likely to have just as many different viewpoints and opinions—but I think it's safe to say that our members, while enjoying spirited debates about some of the details, are generally in line with the perspective outlined in this book.

Like most Americans, Patriotic Millionaires want a tax code that will build the middle class, create good jobs, grow the economy, reward productive citizens and companies, and invest in our future. We want a tax code that reflects the core values of the nation, one that incentivizes people and corporations to do things that are good for the country, and one that pays for what we need and shares those costs fairly.

Unfortunately, not every millionaire wants that kind of tax code. The Other Millionaires actually want to live in a country with a tiny number of rich people, millions of poor people, and no middle class. These Other Millionaires don't want a tax code that "grows the economy"; they want a tax code that grows the economy for them. These Other Millionaires have been spending millions of dollars year after year, contributing to the campaigns of (i.e., paying off) lawmakers to ensure the donut factory makes donuts only for them. These Other Millionaires are not confused about what they are doing—they don't actually believe that tax cuts for them will ever trickle down into the pocketbooks of you and your family. Those are just the words they use to excuse their choices.

In these divided times, with noise and spin coming from every corner of Washington and the media, it's hard to know whom to trust. Taxes are even worse than most other issues, because a lot of politicians actually *want* you to be confused. The less the average person knows about taxes, the easier it is for the rich and powerful to rig the system in their favor.

I am proud to be called a "traitor to my class." Unlike the Other Millionaires, I don't want to live in a country where people can funnel their income through fake Irish corporations to cut their tax bill. I don't want to live in a nation where investors like me have lower tax rates than people who need to work for a living have. I don't want to live in a nation where children like mine (wonderful as my children are) receive millions of dollars in inheritances tax free. Mostly, I don't want to continue to pay low taxes into a system that ensures rich investors like me will get richer and richer while the middle class gets smaller and the poor get even more desperate. And I don't want to live in a system where my fellow millionaires are able to do all those things with impunity.

I want the public to know what's going on behind the scenes. You deserve to know what people are doing to your country and your family just so they can have a few more dollars in their pockets. With what you'll learn in this book, I hope you'll feel empowered to join us in this essential fight. We can win. We have to win. Our future depends on it.

You know, the funny thing is, once we do win, once millionaires across America are paying higher taxes than they ever have, higher taxes than they possibly could have imagined, I think a few of them are going to thank us—for helping them to be rich, in a truly rich country.

Sincerely,
Morris Pearl

# A Note from Erica Payne

Dear Reader,

When I was a little girl growing up in Raleigh, North Carolina, playing with Barbie dolls and dreaming about my future, I never said to myself, When I grow up, I'm going to work on tax policy! Not once.

Even when I started organizing millionaires ten years ago to demand higher taxes on themselves, I didn't think to myself, Now I'm going to work on tax policy! Actually, I might have thought that once, but as soon as I did, I got really depressed and then I fell asleep. Tax policy will do that to you.

Now here I am, ten years later, working on tax policy. Not because I *want* to work on tax policy, but because I want my five-year-old daughter to grow up in a stable, peaceful, and prosperous country. And after years of working in politics and on public policy, wading through the utter nonsense that people and politicians spout to justify their greed and bad choices, I have concluded that the U.S. political economy as it is currently constructed will never—literally never—produce the kind of country that I want my kid to grow up in unless we fix the tax system that undergirds it. (Fellow suburban moms, are you listening?)

There's a reason that rich people and politicians focus most of their attention, their lies, and their behind-the-scenes manipulation on our tax code: it's one of the single most important building blocks of our country's political economy, and it's where "rigging" can generate the highest returns. People think taxes are just the way we pay for things we all need, but our tax system is much more than that.

Our tax system is the primary mechanism through which everything produced in our economy is ultimately divided up. Even small changes to the tax system can have major effects on how the benefits of the economy are dispersed across the population. Whoever controls the tax system controls the distribution. Because millionaires and billionaires and corporate lobbyists currently have the most power in the political arena, they are the ones controlling the tax system and deciding who gets the biggest payout from the economy. They can rig the tax system so it delivers outsized benefits to them, even if it destroys the lives of millions of our people in the process.

Most people understand taxes as the way we pay for things that we decide are easier or better to do together. And because people inevitably disagree about what exactly those things should be, conversations about our tax system invariably turn into arguments about what we should and should not be paying for and who's a freeloader and all that. But just talking about what expenses we should share misses the bigger point.

*Whatever* we decide to do together, those things need to be financed, and the way we finance them matters. (Please note use of *financed* rather than *paid for*! As we'll explain later, the federal budget is not like a state budget or a family budget where there's a direct link between how much money you take in through taxes and how much money you are able to spend on things your citizens need.) Creating a system where those with little to spare are responsible for most of the investment, while those with the most put up the equivalent of nothing, is nuts. It makes much more sense to require the people who have clearly benefited the most from our system to reinvest a huge percentage of their excess wealth back into that system. Please keep in mind that the people we want to tax, the people who are reaping the vast majority of the benefits of our economy, have so much money that taxing them at rates of 70%, 80%, or 90% won't change their lives at all. Don't worry, Ken Griffith; when we're done taxing you, you'll still be able to afford your $238 million New York City apartment, your $122 million mansion near Buckingham Palace, and your $100 million Hamptons estate.[1]

Beyond financing our society's shared priorities, we also use tax policy to encourage and discourage various behaviors. As a parent, I understand incentives and disincentives as well as anyone. If you eat all your vegetables, you can have dessert. If you pull Big Kitty's tail again, you will go for a time-out. The incentives in my household are very clear. The incentives in our tax code are also very clear; they're just dumb.

Did you know that companies that move American jobs to other countries get a tax break? Did you know that our tax code lets people pretend to be businesses so they can get a tax break? Did you know that people who work for the industry that is responsible for millions of layoffs pay a tax rate that's about half of what working people pay? Please read those sentences again. They are true. We've built a system that rewards people for doing all the things we say we don't want them to do. Why? Because politicians aren't working for America;

they're working for their political donors. It's as simple as that. But don't trust me; the politicians have admitted it publicly!

As any parent will tell you, if you reward bad behavior, you're going to get more of it. Thanks to a broken political system, we've been handing out treats to the rich and powerful for so long, they have turned into spoiled brats. I wouldn't deal with this much whining from my five-year-old. Why on earth do we tolerate it from adults who should know better? America's billionaires have gotten to the point where they think they can do whatever they want and still get special treatment. On the rare occasion that someone calls them out on their greed publicly, they go on television and cry about being persecuted. Yes, Steve Schwartzman, we are talking to you. No, paying taxes is not tantamount to the Nazis advancing across Europe.[2] You need a billionaire time-out.

Everything—from how much money you bring home to how good your kid's school is to whether or not you die of COVID-19—is partially dependent on how the economy is structured, and the tax system composes much of the structure of the economy. Providing incentives and disincentives, financing the things we need, fairly splitting the tab—these are not just elements of the country's political economy; they're the primary structural elements of the system that controls almost every aspect of our existence. If the architecture of your house were this faulty—if your house had a framework this unstable—you would not allow your family to sleep there.

Not to be a total downer, but it gets worse. In the last few decades, as our country has gotten more unequal, it has also gotten less stable. If we don't act soon, our future will make

*"Other folks have to pay taxes, too, Mr. Herndon, so would you please spare us the dramatics!"*

the present look like a walk in the park. The mechanism at the center of our shared experience—our *political economy* (remember this term!)—has been purposefully, deliberately designed to produce a country that is less stable, less peaceful, and less prosperous (growing billionaire fortunes notwithstanding). These outcomes are not an accident. This isn't a bug; it's a feature.

I learned in business school that if you execute a bad strategy really well, you fail more quickly than if you execute a bad strategy badly. The people who control how our political economy is structured—mostly politicians and their financial backers—have ensured that our country will become even less stable, less peaceful, and less prosperous *more quickly* over time. The way they have structured our political economy ensures that inequality will continue to increase *at an increasing rate*, accelerating until the whole thing just falls apart under the weight of its own design, like some twisted game of economic Jenga.

What's so sick about it is that the politicians and their financial backers know it. None of this happened by accident. People made it happen. Over time, in a variety of ways, a relatively small group of people systematically restructured our political economy so that it would produce outcomes that were great for them and horrible for everybody else.

For some reason, these people actually want to live in a country with a tiny number of extremely wealthy people, tens of millions of poor people, and no middle class. I don't understand what would make someone want that. I, personally, think that's really weird. I guess some people need to be richer than everyone else in order to be happy. Of course, they don't really seem all that happy, do they? A friend told me once that money can't buy you happiness, but it can buy you a yacht to take you away from unhappiness. Maybe the billionaires manipulating our political system for their own good are just trying to earn enough money to buy a yacht big enough that they can escape all their misery. Good luck with that.

I can't see inside these people's heads, but having spent decades of my life dealing with very rich people, I have concluded that most of this is not actually about money. It's about power. After a certain point where you can afford everything you could ever possibly need, everything you could possibly want, money is no longer just money. It's power.

They say absolute power corrupts absolutely. If money is power, I think it's fair to say that absolute money also corrupts absolutely. You may not have a philosophical problem with someone having an unlimited amount of money, but you should ask yourself whether or not you are comfortable with someone having an unlimited amount of power.

I'm not saying that the rich are necessarily bad people (although one study did show that CEOs are four times more likely to be psychopaths than members of the general population are);[3] I'm just saying you shouldn't trust them to be good people. And given that you're unsure of their moral fiber, it is best to limit both the power they have and the money they have.

Consider the Sackler family, one of the wealthiest families in the country thanks to their ownership of Purdue Pharma. Their wealth gave them an opportunity to be an enormous

force for good. Instead, family members are accused,[4] with Purdue and other manufacturers and distributors, of starting an opioid epidemic that has killed hundreds of thousands of Americans and destroyed the lives of millions more.[5] They did whatever they had to do to get rich and powerful, and millions of people suffered as a result.[6] To add insult to injury, their relentless pursuit of wealth at all costs was aided and abetted by our tax code. The Sacklers ended up even richer for their trouble than they should have because of the tax system our elected leaders wrote.

Morris is right; history should be our guide here. Allowing millionaires and billionaires to control the economy and rig it in their favor doesn't turn out well for anyone, including rich people.

## What You Can Expect from This Book

In this book, we hope to give you the tools and the information you need to join the fight to build a stable America. We won't ever be completely equal, because people naturally have different talents and interests, but we can be less unequal than we are now, both economically and politically, and a little more equal will mean a lot more stable and ultimately more prosperous.

I hope that you will finish this book understanding that the only possible way to fix our country is through taxes. Not charity. Not the private sector or "public-private partnerships." And not "the market," for heaven's sake. Taxes are the only way. Or to quote Dutch historian Rutger Bregman, whose tirade at the World Economic Forum Annual Meeting, in Davos, Switzerland, made him a minor celebrity: "Taxes, taxes, taxes. All the rest is bullshit in my opinion."[7]

There's a scene in the 1993 movie *Searching for Bobby Fischer* where Josh, a child chess protégé, is struggling to find checkmate in a very intense lesson with his teacher, played by Ben Kingsley. The room is palpably silent. "Here, I'll make it easier for you," says Kingsley. With a forceful sweep of his arm, he knocks the chess pieces to the ground with a clatter. "Now look at it," he says. I love that scene. Sometimes we have to clear the board to see the game.

In our complicated world, it can be difficult to see anything, least of all big, structural problems, clearly. There's nothing like a global pandemic, a worldwide recession, an international reckoning on racial injustice, and a looming climate catastrophe to bring about a little clarity. It's as if God swept a celestial arm across humanity's chessboard, hurling the world we understood to the ground. Now look at it. Four moves to checkmate.

That's where we are. And that's why I work on tax policy. Because you can't fix the country without fixing the political economy, and you can't fix the political economy without fixing the tax system.

In five years, the United States of America will turn 250 years old, and I will turn 55. I have been alive for a fifth of my country's entire existence, and the changes that we've gone through in my lifetime have been profound. My five-year-old child will live through a transition of the human experience our wildest dreams can only grasp at. As we approach America's 250th birthday, let's make a commitment. Let's decide that during our second 250 years, we will live up to the promise we were founded on. We can build a fabulous country, a strong, prosperous, and happy place that we will all be proud to leave to our children, if we can just muster the will to tax a bunch of multimillionaires and billionaires. Folks, this is really just not that hard.

I hope that after reading this book, you will decide to work on tax policy too. It's not nearly as boring as it seems and we really need your help. The people screwing everything up are very powerful, and they have a huge amount of money, and we are, after all, just two hundred millionaires. As we sit here today, the Other Millionaires are plotting how to use their money to get more power and how to use their power to get more money. In the process, they are destroying the country that all the rest of us are trying to live in.

Morris and I wrote this book so that normal people without accounting degrees can figure out what's going on and help fix it before it's too late. (Rest assured that while sometimes it feels as if it's already too late, it's not.)

The good news—and maybe the weirdest part of it all— is that fixing what's wrong is not particularly difficult. The Other Millionaires make it seem complicated on purpose so that people feel powerless to change things. But it isn't, and we aren't.

Tax the rich; save America. Let's get started.

Erica Payne
President and founder of the Patriotic Millionaires

# TAX THE RICH!

# What Exactly Is "Rich"? (by Erica)

*If I had a million dollars, we wouldn't have to walk to the store.*
*. . . we'd take a limousine 'cause it costs more. . .*
*If I had a million dollars . . . I'd be rich.*

          —Barenaked Ladies

---

If you're going to write a book called *Tax the Rich!* (much less run an entire organization focused on taxing the rich), at some point or another you better be prepared to answer the question, What exactly do you mean by *rich*? Like beauty, rich is often in the eye of the beholder. And no one has more opinions about what rich is than rich people.

The Patriotic Millionaires organization defines *rich* as people with incomes of $1 million and/or assets of $5 million. (We'll talk more about incomes vs. assets later.) In order to become a member of the Patriotic Millionaires, you have to have at least that much money, and we focus our work exclusively on taxing people with that much money or more.

The technical, dictionary definition of a *millionaire* is someone with a net worth of at least $1 million. If, for example, you make $250,000 a year, have $10,000 in your checking account, $500,000 in your retirement account, and owe the bank $500,000 on the mortgage of your $1 million home, you are a millionaire. Congratulations! Good for you. We still don't think you are rich (no offense), and we do not want you to pay higher taxes.

If, however, you make $1 million a year in income, have $1 million in your E*TRADE account, and own two houses (just you, not you and the bank), each worth $2 million, we do think that you are rich. Not as rich as Bill Gates, certainly, but rich enough that you should pay higher taxes and not gripe about it.

The whole question of what is rich and who should pay higher taxes came up right at the beginning of the Patriotic Millionaires. The group first came together in 2010 during the lame-duck session of Congress when it became clear that President Obama was going to cave to Republican demands to extend the Bush tax cuts, including those for the richest taxpayers. I found it incredibly offensive that a Democratic president would even consider lowering taxes on the richest Americans, and I wanted to call him out on it publicly.

I worked with two millionaires (one lawyer and one retired Google engineer) to craft a letter to President Obama and other elected leaders that said, simply, For the good of the country, raise our taxes. We asked people with incomes of $1 million and/or assets of $5 million to sign the letter, planning to release it when we had a good number of signatures. As we circulated it among wealthy people we knew and people we knew who might know wealthy people, the angry phone calls started pouring in. Progressives were furious that we had "moved the goalpost" by defining *rich* at such a high level. Weren't people making $600,000 or $700,000 a year also rich? Did we really think they shouldn't pay higher taxes? Who the hell did we think we were? Had these millionaires lost all perspective?

Maybe. I blame it on a makeup lady at Fox. In the middle of circulating the letter and fielding all these angry phone calls, I was called in for an appearance on Fox News. Fox hosts love yelling at liberals, and I love getting my hair and makeup done by a professional, so it was a pretty good trade. Anyway, all these progressives were yelling at me, so I decided to do a mini–focus group with the Fox makeup lady as she glued on my fake eyelashes, one by one. I figured she wasn't wealthy herself, and I knew she watched Fox News all day, so I was curious about her perspective.

I asked her, Did she think that people making $250,000 a year should pay higher taxes? Her answer? An emphatic no. If you live in New York City and have kids, that's not that much money, she explained. I tried again at $400,000. Still no. She said someone may be living in New York City, have kids, and also be taking care of aging parents; they clearly cannot afford higher taxes, she insisted. And so it continued at various levels—$500,000, $600,000, $700,000. At each level, the Fox makeup lady was unwilling to impose higher taxes. Until I got to $1 million. No hesitation. They can pay higher taxes, she said. Case closed.

This conversation was really instructive for me in terms of marketing the idea of raising taxes on the wealthy, and I

"I'm combing our finances for all this disposable income I keep reading we have."

think politicians would do well to take notice—the gray area on this tax debate is costing you big time. Generally speaking, the left's position in the tax argument is that anyone making $250,000 a year or more should be paying higher taxes. And ultimately the deal that Obama cut with Republicans ended the Bush tax cuts for single people making more than $400,000 and couples making more than $450,000 a year. During the 2020 campaign, Biden embraced a similarly centrist position, laying out a plan to start raising taxes at around the $400,000 level.[1]

Now, I personally agree with the further left position on this. I make around $250,000 a year, and, as I said earlier, I would be perfectly happy to pay higher taxes, especially if it meant I didn't have to pay $30,000 a year for day care. (Thank goodness my kid finally started public school.) Frankly, I just don't think that much about my personal tax bill. Once a year, my accountant sends me a stack of papers to sign, and one of those pages has a big number on it that reflects how much money I sent to the government. Each year, I look at that number and think, Damn, that's a lot of money. Then I sign on the dotted line and don't think about it again until the next year.

Clearly, not everyone is as lackadaisical about the whole thing as I am. During the 2016 election, an old friend of mine explained that she was voting for Donald Trump because she knew that if he won, she would pay lower taxes. Paying lower taxes is very important to her. She had just written a $200,000 check to the IRS for her 2015 taxes, and the very act of writing that check resolved her indecision and convinced her to vote for Trump, even though she had voted for Obama in the previous two elections.

Now, you may think, Wow, $200,000 is a lot of money. It *is* a lot of money, particularly when that money used to be in your checking account, and now it isn't. But there's more to this story. You see, my friend doesn't work, never really has worked, and certainly never plans to work in the future if she can possibly avoid it. Her dad left her a lot of money when he died, and she has been living off the investment income from that inheritance ever since. Given that the tax rate on long-term capital gains is lower than the rate on ordinary income, her $200,000 tax bill likely reflected an income of around $1 million, right at the point the Patriotic Millionaires define as rich.

Should my friend have been upset about her tax bill? Is she paying too much? Too little? Would your answer change if she had made that money working at a job instead of inheriting it? Ask yourself these questions again when you have finished reading this book, and see if your answers change.

The real point here is that rich means different things to different people. It may even mean different things to the same people at different times. I can't tell you how many conversations I have had with rich people about how poor they are. The stock market falls a few points and "Cry Me A River" starts playing on a loop on Tesla radios everywhere.

A friend of mine lives in Haiti, where she's a school administrator during the day and a mother to thirteen orphans at night. To her, I'm rich. To those orphans, she is rich. To the children on the streets of Haiti, those thirteen orphans are rich.

So, there's *relatively* rich—rich as compared with others—and then there's "Are you kidding me?!" rich like Jeff Bezos, Bill Gates, and Mark Zuckerberg. A member of the Patriotic Millionaires calls this group the Three Amigos, a reference to the 1986 comedy where Steve Martin, Chevy Chase, and Martin Short are mistaken for real-life heroes. (See the parallel?) The wealth of the Three Amigos (Jeff, Bill, and Mark, not Steve, Chevy, and Martin) is greater than the total wealth of the entire bottom half of the U.S. population. Those three men own more than is owned collectively by 160 million of their fellow Americans (so this reboot is more tragedy than comedy).[2]

Jeff Bezos is so rich that he kept the top spot even after giving ex-wife MacKenzie Scott a quarter of his Amazon stock. Imagine that: you just gave away 25% of your stake in your company, and you are still the richest person on the entire planet, in fact, the richest human who has ever lived in history. Now, that's rich. I hope we can at least agree on that.

It's really hard to even comprehend how rich these three men are. The human brain isn't built to translate that many zeros into any coherent understanding of wealth. Here's some context:

- If you had worked every single day from the time Columbus sailed to America to the present and earned $5,000 per day, you would still have less money than Jeff Bezos makes in a week.

# The wealthiest three Americans now have more wealth than the bottom half of the country combined.

**You are closer to being homeless than you ever will be to being a billionaire.**

$0

$60,000
Middle Class

$185,000,000,000
Jeff Bezos

- If you had made $100,000 every single day since the year 1 A.D. and saved every penny, you would still have less money than Bill Gates has.
- If you had started working when the human race, *Homo sapiens*, first walked upright, around two hundred thousand years ago, and saved $100,000 a year, you would still not have as much money as Mark Zuckerberg has.

Now, there are a whole lot of zeros separating the Three Amigos from my poor friend trying to scrape by on a measly million bucks a year. And can we please take a moment here to offer our deepest sympathies to the 221 American billionaires who were not quite rich enough to make the cut of the Forbes 400? So sorry, Sheryl Sandberg; perhaps you should have "leaned in" a little harder. In 2019, the price of admission to the Forbes 400, the most exclusive club in America, was $2 billion. The combined net worth of the members of the Forbes 400 in 2019 was up 2% from the year before, reaching $2.96 trillion, more than the gross domestic product (GDP) of the United Kingdom.[3]

So many zeros. It's hard to get your head around it. Even with as much time as I have spent around the millionaire class, I still can't really grasp all those zeros. When I was growing up, rich meant that your parents belonged to the Carolina Country Club and that you got a new car for your sixteenth birthday (probably a Jeep Cherokee). Rich meant that you had lots of beads on your Add-A-Bead and that you had actually eaten at the Angus Barn, rather than just driven past it wondering what it looked like inside. Rich meant that your father wore a suit at work and your mother wore silk blouses at home. Rich meant that your house was perpetually tidy and smelled of Lemon Pledge. Then I moved to Washington, DC, and realized I didn't know what rich was. Not even close.

# When Is a Dollar More—or Much Less—Than a Dollar: The Marginal Utility of Money (by Morris)

*I love money. I love everything about it. I bought some pretty good stuff. Got me a $300 pair of socks. Got a fur sink. An electric dog polisher. A gasoline powered turtleneck sweater. And, of course, I bought some dumb stuff, too.*

—Steve Martin

Comedian Steve Martin clearly gets one of my favorite concepts in economics called the marginal utility of money. Some people just have so much money that they need to find ridiculous ways to spend it like gold plating their living room. The marginal utility of money is a simple but kind of mind-blowing concept that says that the more money you have, the less valuable each additional dollar is to you. At a certain point, when you have enough dollars, each additional dollar is worth essentially nothing to you. Zero. Nada. Let me explain.

Say you're a student who has $100 in your checking account. If someone gives you $100, that's a huge windfall. You've doubled your money, and that extra $100 can do a lot for you—pay bills, buy books (well, considering college-textbook prices, more like half a book), or purchase groceries.

On the other hand, if you're a millionaire like me, that money means basically nothing to you. A few months ago, I was reorganizing some stuff and found a few hundred-dollar bills I had put in my camera case when traveling in the French West Indies a few years ago. Finding that extra few hundred did not change my life at all. There's nothing that I'm not doing for a lack of a hundred dollars. It clearly meant so little to me that I didn't even know I had lost it.

Imagine you had just found a few hundred dollars. How would you feel? Would it make a big difference in your life or no difference at all? Maybe somewhere in the middle?

That amount of money means much less to me than it does to the student. Its "marginal utility" is much lower for me than it is for the student. The marginal utility just means the incremental additional use I would get out of one dollar compared to the incremental use I got out of the previous dollar and the one before that.

Think of pizza. If you are really hungry and someone orders a pizza, that pizza likely means quite a bit to you; each delicious cheesy bite fills you up a bit more until you're no longer hungry. Imagine you ate the entire pizza and were so full that you had to unbutton the top button of your pants just to be comfortable. Now imagine that just after you loosened your pants, someone ordered another pizza. You might eat a little more, even though you are already full, or you might put some away in the refrigerator to eat later. Then someone orders still another pizza. Maybe you will freeze this one and the one after that. You probably don't like the additional pizzas as much as you liked that first one, but you are glad to have those frozen pizzas in case you need a late-night snack. Now say someone ordered you several million pizzas.

As someone who is living on millions of dollars in investments, the marginal utility of any additional dollar—like those extra pizzas—to me is almost zero. I am almost uncomfortable typing this because it sounds so obnoxious. But I want you to understand. The people we want to tax have obnoxious amounts of money—so much that even if someone handed them an additional $101,800 (the median net worth of every household in America),[4] their life wouldn't change *at all*. The people we want to tax the most have so much money that if we handed them $1 million, they still wouldn't notice it. They can't even think about money in a practical way anymore because there's no way for them realistically to spend it all in their lifetime. It's all abstract numbers with no effect on their lives whatsoever. They already have as many homes, as many jets, as many clothes, and as many sponsorships of the ballet as someone can enjoy in one lifetime. Their wealth reaches a point where money isn't even real to them anymore. It's not that it doesn't have value; it's that it doesn't have value *to them*. And we should try really hard to understand this when we discuss our tax system.

For people making $400,000, $500,000, even $600,000, money is still real; that's not the case for people who make $10 million or $20 million a year. And it is certainly not the case for people who have one thousand million dollars (a.k.a. $1 billion). Congresswoman Alexandria Ocasio-Cortes set the internet on fire when she called for 70% tax rates on incomes over $10 million (meaning that someone would pay 70% starting with the first dollar of the eleventh million). She was taking into account the marginal utility of money. That eleventh million just doesn't provide much value to a person who already has $10 million. If you are still confused about the concept, don't eat all day long and then at 9 p.m. order yourself a pizza. Once you've eaten that pizza, order twenty more, and see if they make you as happy as that first pizza. If you have no dollars and someone gives you $1 million dollars, I guarantee you are way happier about that first million than the other person is about the eleventh million.

## When Is $1,000 More Than $1 Million?

But what does that have to do with taxes? Well, the same principle applies. The more money you have, the less valuable it is to you. Let's consider the flat tax. Rich people love talking about how we should have a flat tax so we can all be equal. But what does their kind of equality really mean? Let's say we implement a 5% flat tax rate for all income earners regardless of how much money they make. In this scenario, someone making $20,000 would pay $1,000, and someone making $20 million would pay $1 million. Now, 5% of $20,000 ($1,000) is much less than 5% of $20 million ($1 million), but to the person making $20,000, that extra $1,000 means rent, food, heat, and transportation. To the person with $19 million, that extra $1 million means almost nothing. Okay, perhaps a new yacht.

Most Americans do not have an extra $1,000. One study showed that 40% of Americans couldn't come up with $400 in an emergency. A thousand dollars is a huge amount of money to someone with very little. A million dollars is not a lot of money to someone with nineteen million other dollars. That

"I've been thinking about the flat tax and how it would inflict hardship on the poor, and I can live with that."

$1,000 has much more use in the life of someone struggling to get by—a higher marginal utility—than the $1 million does to the millionaire, who already has those things and more covered. Sorry, Steve Forbes, the flat tax is just flat dumb.

For a regular person, it can be hard to comprehend the idea that $1 million, $2 million, even $200 million may have absolutely no material effect on someone's life. So what is it that all these millionaires and billionaires are fighting about, given that, for all intents and purposes, the money in question has no value in their lives whatsoever? Bragging rights at the golf club?

Let's hear what a few of the Patriotic Millionaires have to say about what "rich" is.

"If I won the lottery, I would go on living as I always did."

## Straight from the Horse's Mouth:
## What Patriotic Millionaires Think "Rich" Is

Kristin Luck: Serial marketing-technology entrepreneur and founder/managing partner of ScaleHouse

❝ *I grew up poor in rural Oregon. Poor as in receiving-government-food-boxes poor. After I graduated from university, which I paid for through a combination of grants, student loans, and full-time work, I moved to Los Angeles. During the interview for my first corporate job in LA, the CEO asked me how much money I would need to earn annually in order to feel like I had really "made it." The biggest number I could ever imagine earning was $55,000, so I blurted it out. He managed not to laugh. Within a few years, I had hit my goal before going on to start and sell a succession of companies that would create (if managed correctly) a lifetime of financial security.*

*I think there's a path for "new money" folks, and mine was pretty typical. In my early thirties, I bought a house right out-side Hollywood and a high-end sports car. I flew first class and stayed exclusively at five-star hotels. But after a while, the lifestyle started to wear on me. I missed my family in Oregon, and I was exhausted from working constantly. I wasn't finding a lot of joy in day-to-day living. But the beautiful thing about being human is that we have the capacity to grow and learn, and as we age, we gain a deeper understanding of what we truly value.*

*In my late forties, 'rich' has a much different meaning than it did in my thirties. I drive a fifteen-year old car and live down an unassuming gravel road. I value autonomy above all else, and*

*being rich gives me that. It allows me to live, unbothered, in a small Oregon town and enjoy wild spaces. I can support causes I'm passionate about and protect the people and places I love. I have access to fresh food and the time to feed myself and my soul. I can travel and explore the world on my own terms. I'm able to be selective and take on work that excites and inspires me and through which I feel I can truly make an impact. This is what rich is to me.* "

## John Deane: Founder of Southwind Health Partners, a physician practice management and consulting firm

" *Recently I experienced my second multimillion-dollar payout after selling my company twice: once to the original acquirer and again when the original acquirer was itself acquired ten years later. In light of that wildly successful year, my wife and I decided to retire and help out others. We invested in a small boutique resort and marina, jumping on an opportunity to build a business in a part of rural Tennessee that needed an economic boost.*

*At the end of that year, I sat down with my tax accountant, who told me that the federal income tax liability for my record year of income was only 3.5%, thanks, of course, to the provision in the Trump tax bill called accelerated depreciation. I was completely floored. I'd finally made it!*

*That's what being rich means to me—finally experiencing firsthand how the system is built to favor the rich and make them richer. It means being asked to give back less when you've just made more than ever. It means getting great personal news at a time when working Americans are falling deeper into poverty each day, and it just makes me sad.* **》》**

## Jacqueline Boberg: Silicon Valley start-up beneficiary

**《《** *I can remember exactly when I decided I wanted to become rich. I was working in London, my hometown, in the 1970s, and the jobs I had took me to very affluent areas across London, such as Mayfair, Kensington, and Hampstead. I looked around and saw what appeared to me to be happy people going into the kinds of restaurants and stores that I had no access to, with all this free time I never had. However, I did have access to national health care, free higher education, and good public transportation. Zoom ahead twenty-five years, and I now occupy a world of wealth I had only ever dreamed of.*

*It's become clear to me that wealth isn't about going to nice restaurants or fancy stores but about having access to every level of society and any number of special privileges. In the United States, it means having access to all the health care I can pay for, access to excellent schools and colleges for my children, and access to influencing the political class through donations. Wealth is having access to an existence free from worry about where my next mortgage, health care, or credit-card payment is coming from. But having that access is unequally distributed, and I don't want to live on my privileged island of wealth surrounded by a sea of inequality. It isn't good for me, and it isn't good for the people living without access to basic needs just so that I can grow my portfolio beyond my wildest dreams and live in a country that mints the most billionaires in the world.* **》》**

## Michael Lambert: Former boat builder, married into wealth

**❝** *For most people, everything between having $1 million and Jeff Bezos's $188 billion would be considered rich. In fact, before I became wealthy, a friend expressed shock that I had saved $8,000, so trying to define the word 'wealthy' is an amorphous target. But I believe that at some level of wealth, there is what I call 'the point of no escape.' That point is when the income from investments exceeds the cost of living for what most would call a wealthy lifestyle—basically, when you can live that lifestyle without working at all. If you had, say, $188 million, you could easily afford multiple large houses, a big yacht, a plane, and anything else you could dream of without ever working a day in your life. To illustrate how large a range the idea of rich covers, it just so happens that Jeff Bezos has enough money for one thousand people to live that lifestyle. But then again, if you have 'only' $20 million, you'd make around $1 million per year from investments, which should be enough for anyone.* **❞**

## Eric Klose: Former tech executive, current angel investor

**❝** *What does something cost? For me, I've always thought of it in terms of what I'd have to give up—which usually is nothing. A new car might cost me $60,000, but buying something like that just moves some numbers around in my bank account. I have enough money that I don't need to think about it. I don't have to skip a vacation, stop eating out, or even delay purchasing a new appliance for my home in order to make a monthly payment, as so many currently do. The same thing goes for my taxes. If you raise my taxes by 10%, of course I'll have less money, but what does it* *cost? My lifestyle or my spending doesn't have to change. Because I'm not sacrificing anything to accommodate it, it doesn't cost me a thing.* »

## Rick Feldman: Broadcast TV station executive

« *'Rich' is a relative term. Around the globe, there are instances where owning shoes, running water, or a cow would make one rich.*

*But as a white male born in the United States after World War II, I was lucky because I was born rich. I don't mean literally. I was rich because I was born in a time and place where opportunity was in abundance.*

*Rich is the ability to live your life as you want. That may include a desire for significant monetary wealth or to be content with 'enough.' It means a roof over your head, a decent education, food to eat, and the opportunity to follow your dreams with enough space to make a mistake or two. It offers the security of not having to always worry. After all, the wealthier you are, the more the world opens up to you and, with it, increased possibilities and opportunities to build the 'rich' life you aspire to.*

*It's true that money does not bring happiness, but that is because, for some people, nothing will. For the rest of us, the peace that comes with not being forced to worry about money is what makes us rich.* »

## Alan Davis: Investor, heir, and founder and president of Conservatree paper company

« *Many people still think of rich in twentieth-century terms, before the explosive growth in income and wealth inequality that went into high gear at the beginning of this century. In the old days, we referred to the top 1% as rich. No more. The 1% are merely affluent, whereas the top 0.1% are rich. In fact, the top 0.1% are so rich that there are now four categories of rich.*

*The bottom of the 0.1% starts at approximately $25 million in net worth and/or $2.5 million in annual income, approximately five times greater than the 1% threshold. But higher up the food chain within the 0.1% class are billionaires—650 of them in the United States. This is forty times greater than the poorest of the 0.1%.*

*Above the billionaires is the unique club known as the Forbes 400, America's 400 richest people. Their wealth starts at about $2.5 billion. Imagine how tragic it must be for the 250 billionaires who cross this incredible billionaire finish line and can't even make the Forbes list!*

*And then there are the centibillionaires, and in case you don't know what that looks like, it's $100,000,000,000. They have more than one hundred times more money than entry-class billionaires. They are the 0.1% of billionaires but have 20% of all billionaire wealth.*

*Rich is not in the eye of the beholder. Rich is the top 0.1%. Accept it and then we can do something about it.* **”**

## Lawrence B. Benenson: Principal, Benenson Capital Partners

**“** *Rich is: not knowing how to read a balance sheet.*

*Rich is: not knowing if doctor's bills have been reimbursed by health insurance.*

*Rich is: having vacation houses that are visited a few months out of the year.*

*Rich is: belonging to country clubs and not going to them for years.*

*Rich is: getting lots of great publicity for signing the Giving Pledge, but not giving away half your money before you die because how do you know when you're going to die?*

*Rich is: starting a charitable foundation and spending 40% of the 5% of the foundation's assets you're required to spend annually on paying relatives for meaningless jobs, going to conferences, and having fancy office space.*

*Rich is: earning at least 5% on one's money for one's charitable foundation and therefore keeping 95% in a bank or investments in perpetuity so that money never goes to finding a cure or helping the poor.*

*Rich is: leaving your hotel for days at a time, but not checking out.*

*Rich is: hiring tax lawyers to avoid, but not evade, taxes.*

*Rich is: having estate lawyers to avoid, but not evade, estate taxes.*

*Rich is: voting for people who give tax breaks to rich people.*

*Rich is: not knowing how to turn off the water in your house.*

*Rich is: buying foreign cars but complaining about the trade deficit.* **"**

## Morris Pearl: Former managing director at BlackRock

**"** *My late father-in-law (Louis Lowenstein, who was a founder of the law firm now known as Kramer Levin and later was the CEO* *of Pathmark) used to say that the purpose of having money is to not have to think about money.*

*And that is what I think being 'rich' really means. It means never not doing something because of a lack of money.*

*I don't mean I waste money. When I go to the grocery store and the Barilla penne in the red and blue box is $1.79 and the De Cecco penne in the yellow and blue box is $3.49, I usually get the red and blue box. But if there aren't any left, I get the yellow and blue box without thinking about it.*

*But to be more serious, to me, 'rich' means:*

- *My young-adult children decide what to do based on what interests them the most and how they feel they can make the world better, because they don't have to worry about loan payments or living expenses.*
- *My doctor finds the best specialist to deal with my condition, knowing that I don't care whether they take insurance or how much the bill will be.*
- *My major accomplishment was that by the time my children were old enough to understand that they could live frugally on their trust funds and never work, they were mature enough not to want that life.*
- *The difficult conversation about money with my son was when he was five and I tried to explain to him that it was ridiculous to get a car service to bring us where even he could walk in a minute or two.*

*And I don't mean to imply that the challenges of being rich are anything comparable to the challenges of not having enough money. That is my whole point—that they are not. I'm still a nor-mal human being with problems and challenges to overcome, but I can be reasonably sure that none of those problems is going to be the result of my not having enough money to avoid it.*

*That security gives me the freedom to do a lot of other things in my life that I might want to do, such as quit my job and devote myself full-time to political activism. If I had spent most of my working years in a minimum-wage job, I wouldn't have anywhere near enough saved up to stop working. At its core, being rich is about doing what I want without worrying about money.* **"**

# WTF Is the "Economy," and Why Do the People Who Wrote This Book Keep Calling It the "Political Economy"? (by Erica)

The next time some TV pundit tells you that corporate profits are up and the stock market is up and that means the economy is doing great, please throw something at your TV, yell "Liar!" at the top of your lungs, and then rage-tweet @MariaBartiromo, Wall Street's "Money Honey."

Rich people really care about the stock market, and advertisers really care about rich people. As a result, there is a huge amount of advertising money available to support media programming focused on the stock market, corporate profits, and related subjects (including, but not limited to, the great wisdom of America's CEOs). All of that seems like economic reporting, but it isn't really.

It's easy to see how people get confused and start believing that if the stock market is doing well, that must mean the economy is doing well, which must mean that their personal economy (the economy you experience in your daily life—wages, cost of living) will start doing well soon too . . . any day now. It actually doesn't mean that at all. The stock market is just a collection of companies, so if the profits of those companies are up, the stock prices of those companies are up, which means the people who own that stock are richer (at least on paper). It doesn't necessarily have anything to do with "the economy" writ large.

Maybe those high profits mean the companies are selling amazing products to satisfied customers every day as they expand their workforce and enhance their human capital. Fabulous. But maybe, instead, those corporations are recording record profits not because they are selling more products but because last quarter they slashed the pay of everyone who works for them, substituted a crappy product for the good one, upped their advertising a bit, and hoped no one noticed.

That's good (at least in the short term) for the rich people who own stock that has just gone up and bad (at least in the short term) for the working people who needed those paychecks to support their families and who don't own stock (or at least not very much of it). And it's potentially very bad for someone harmed by the inferior product, but we'll leave that discussion for another day.

Titans of industry and Wall Street insist that working people suffering in the short term is a good thing because in the long term the economy will adjust, and everyone will be better off. And advertisers who love rich people provide an enormous amount of funding for programming that focuses on

"I feel so good today I could almost turn down a tax cut."

how the economy is performing for this specific segment of the population, in addition to highlighting the incredible wisdom of these mighty leaders. Lucky us!

Essentially all the economic gains of the last twenty years have gone to a tiny sliver of the wealthiest Americans, and that's not by accident or divine right, and it certainly isn't because rich people are *better* than everybody else. It's by design. The wealthy have paid for the ability to stand at the drawing board and plan out big parts of the economy so that the whole thing works particularly well for them. They've built a factory specially designed to deliver the finished product only to the people who designed the factory. Not an economy that works, but one that works *for them*.

If you put this book down and remember only one thing from its many engaging pages, please remember this:

## The Economy Is Constructed by Human Beings

Right now, the economy is delivering most of its gains to an increasingly small group of people who are already incredibly wealthy and just happen to have a huge amount of influence in the political arena. I'm shocked, I tell you, shocked. How on earth did this happen?

Well. That's the trick. This didn't "just happen"; a small group of very wealthy people spent a huge amount of money over a very long period of time to influence a political system to write tax laws to ensure that the economy would deliver most of its gains to them. They designed a system that ensured they would control a growing portion of the mechanism that

"Making money's even more of a kick when no one else is."

controls our economy—the tax system—and, in so doing, assure that basically whatever happened, they would keep on getting richer.

You may wonder what we mean by "structure the economy." Isn't that what communists do? you wonder. I thought we had a free market. What in the world are you talking about?

First of all, people talk about the economy as if it were a person. We talk about the health of the economy, the strength of the economy. My friend Anat Shenker-Osorio wrote a whole book about the language people use to talk about the economy and how that has a significant effect on how we think about it. I will trust you to read *Don't Buy It: The Trouble with Talking Nonsense about the Economy* on your own, but for this book's purposes, let's just start with the idea that the economy is *not* a person. And even thinking about the economy as a free-standing entity that has agency or the ability to move around on its own will get you into all kinds of trouble. Consider statements such as "The economy is healthy" and "Don't tax the rich, you might hurt the economy's recovery." They talk as if the economy were your Aunt Sally just off chemo and needing a rest. Newsflash, the economy is not your Aunt Sally.

A much better way to understand the economy is to think of it as a giant piece of complex machinery, such as a car. If it's running hot or smoking, you change a valve. You see what happens and then fix another part until the engine works as you want it to. The economy is like that, a giant machine with a million moving parts, some of which are controlled by "markets" (meaning, just lots of people making decisions about what they want and what they are willing to pay for it) and some of which are controlled by the government (such as whether or not it's legal for a company to dump pollution into a lake or allow an eight-year-old to work in a coal mine). There are billions of different pieces that influence the economy, but the most important thing to understand is that like any other machine, the economy is built by human hands.

Morris is a computer guy. He used to write programs that would translate vast amounts of data into actionable information. Among other things, during the 2008 financial crisis, when the government needed to figure out the cost of the bank bailout, Morris designed a system to analyze the auto-industry exposure, from every outstanding car loan to the credit cards that the executives of all the car companies carried. Vast lines of code translated all that data into digestible information that regulators could use to figure out how to navigate the crisis.

The economy is like that. It is constructed, like lines of code or a big complex machine. And, crucially, much of that code is controlled by human beings.

## But What Actually *Is* the Economy?

Let's back up a little further and understand exactly what the economy *is*. The *Encyclopedia Britannica*, reigning queen of basic information (sorry, Wikipedia), puts it this way: an economic system is "any of the ways in which humankind has arranged for its material provisioning."[1] Hmm, okay, perhaps a bit more detail. Investopedia says the economy is "the large set of interrelated production and consumption activities that aid in determining how scarce resources are allocated. In an economy, the production and consumption of goods and services are used to fulfill the needs of those living and operating within it."[2]

Now we're getting somewhere. The economy is just all the millions of activities—making, selling, buying, and trading things—that humans do to ensure that we have what we need, that we have enough "provisions." That seems pretty straightforward. And it means an economy has two distinct tasks: producing as many necessary goods and services as possible, and dividing them up among people effectively. That's it. At its core, an economy or an economic *system* is just the method by which societies or governments produce, organize, and distribute goods and services to all the people in a specific region. So if you want to know how well any economy is doing, you should consider how well or poorly that economic system is producing and distributing resources for the people who live within it.

With that context in mind, how well is our economy working? How well is it utilizing its finite resources to produce and distribute the things the people who live here need? Considering those questions, we must admit that our economy is not working well at all, and it hasn't worked well for a while.

## Our Rigged Economy

The Patriotic Millionaires held their Tax the Rich! conference in April 2019, months before almost anyone in the world had ever heard of COVID-19. At the time, 40% of Americans said they couldn't come up with $400 in an emergency, and yet we had more billionaires than we'd ever had, and those billionaires were richer than they'd ever been.[3] Our economy was working so badly before the coronavirus that the disparity between rich and poor was higher in the United States than in almost any other developed country, and it was higher than it had been in the United States in almost one hundred years.[4]

The toll this inequality-producing economic machine was taking on our people was enormous. In 2019, more than 2.5 million people were addicted to opioids.[5] Deaths of despair—deaths due to alcohol, drugs, and suicide—were at the highest point ever recorded, and for the first time in our country's history, life expectancy was going down for segments of our population.[6] Once COVID-19 took hold, we saw exactly how rigged our economy is. In the first six months of the pandemic, 30 million people lost their jobs, and America's billionaires made $845 billion dollars (yes, that's a "b").

This epidemic of deaths and drug addiction didn't just happen. The economy didn't wake up one day and decide to start shooting up our people with heroin and killing them. Remember, it's a machine, not a person. Instead, what happened is that over time human beings made big and small changes to our economic system so that our society became more and more unequal. A few people got everything the factory was making; many got nothing, and a lot of people started to think that they may never get anything from the factory at all. The societal results of this economy are clear.

You can't really argue with the results. You might not like them, but they are irrefutable. Our economy—our current

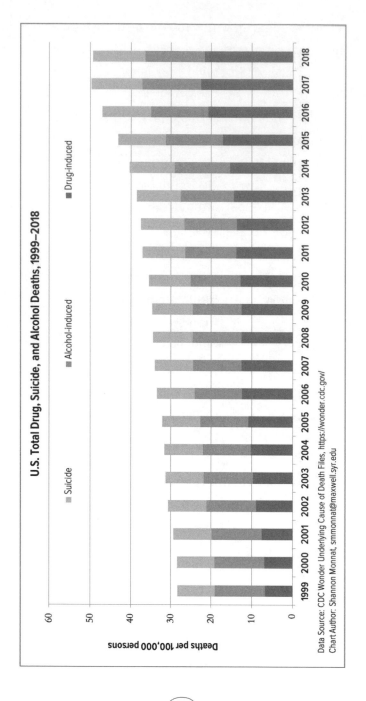

Data Source: CDC Wonder Underlying Cause of Death Files, https://wonder.cdc.gov/
Chart Author: Shannon Monnat, smmonnat@maxwell.syr.edu

economic system—does not allocate our finite resources in a way that fulfills the needs of the people living here.

Now, interestingly, despite how many different kinds of people and cultures there are in the world, there are only four kinds of economic systems:

- a traditional economic system, which is the oldest type and is usually based on hunting or agriculture;
- a command economic system, where a dominant authority—usually the government—makes most of the production and distribution decisions;
- a market economic system, where there is no government involvement and markets are "free"; and
- a mixed economic system, which is a combination of a market economy and a command economy.

There are no pure free-market systems in the world today, and there haven't really ever been any in the modern era, aside from failed states and black markets. The United States and most other Western countries have mixed economic systems—basically, capitalism with varying levels of government-enforced rules.

Now let's return to the beginning and put it all together. According to what we've learned, the U.S. economy is the combination of all the production and consumption in the United States, a set of interrelated activities that divide up finite resources through a combination of the free market and government action in order to fulfill (or fail to fulfill) the needs of the people living here. Got it.

## Why We Should Call It the "Political" Economy

Okay, our economy is increasingly generating more billionaires, more people who can't come up with $400 in an emergency, more addicted people, and more dead people . . . and that was before COVID-19. Why is it doing that? Simple. It's doing it because that is what it was designed to do by the people who control the design.

Most of the time when people are talking about the economy, it would be more accurate to call it the *political economy*, or how a nation's politics control the nation's economy.

Both the decisions being made about how the economy is structured and the process for how we determine who controls those decisions are inherently political, meaning that they are decided within the political arena. We cannot divorce the economy from politics; one creates the other. They are inextricably linked.

Every government decision, from deregulating derivatives to raising the minimum wage, is made in the political arena, and every one of those decisions affects the economy's structure, how it functions, and what results it produces. Picture someone standing inside a giant machine with a wrench in their hand. Here they are tightening a valve, replacing a hose, greasing a gear. All those things affect how the machine works, what it does with inputs to turn them into outputs. The machine doesn't decide to replace its own carburetor; people do that. And that changes the way the economy functions. It changes the way that the scarce resources are turned into

"Congratulations, sire—your financial reforms have been successful!"

goods and services, and allocated to fulfill the needs of the people in that arena.

If we want to start reallocating those goods and services more effectively, what we really need to do is replace the people changing the valves—our elected mechanics. But first let's understand a little more about how the whole thing works. How exactly do you structure an economy, and how does someone go about rigging an economy in their own favor? Here's a hint: they start with the tax code.

# How to Rig an Economy (by Morris)

*My daddy always said: if you can't get in the front door,*
*just go around to the back.*

—J.R. Ewing

In 2017, President Trump and Republican lawmakers rewrote the entire federal tax code. With control of the White house, the Senate, and the House of Representatives, the Republican Party had a chance to write and pass their very best ideas into law. They passed the massive Tax Cuts and Jobs Act along a strict party-line vote. Almost every Republican voted for the new tax code. Every single Democrat voted against it.

Republicans had the power, and with it they created their ideal tax system. They had so much political power that they really didn't have to compromise on anything. This is actually quite lucky for our book because it makes it very easy to see the distinction between the two sides. Or at least it makes it very easy to see what sort of tax structure the Republican

"Under the new tax plan, do we get it in the neck
more or less than under the old tax plan?"

Party wants. It's all there in black and white, in lines and lines of text in a bill that is now the law of the land.

The other side, the Democratic side, is still a moving target (to say the least). Democrats from Bernie Sanders to Joe Biden have called for higher taxes on the wealthy to varying degrees, but what kind of tax system Democrats would actually pass if they were to have as much political power as the Republicans had in 2017 remains to be seen. In the meantime, it's quite helpful to be able to see at least one side of the debate clearly, and to hear what the other side insists it will do differently, if only given the chance. Unfortunately, much of what's wrong with the tax code is built into the whole culture of Washington, not just one party. Regardless, if the Republican Tax Cuts and Jobs Act of 2017 did one thing, it brought clarity to a muddy puddle, so let's start there.

Like all tax codes, the new Republican tax code encourages some things and discourages others. It makes a determination about how much money the federal government needs to finance its activities and divides up the bill among us. It makes a distinction between various income levels (remember the marginal utility of money!), grouping us according to how much extra income we have to contribute to the community pot. It defines countless pieces of our economic engine, from what small businesses can consider expenses when calculating profits, all the way up to guiding how U.S. companies function in the global tax system.

Politicians really like to talk about what their ideas are going to do in the future, but in the next few pages, I want to talk about what the new Republican tax code is doing right now. Once you have read this section, you should think about whether or not you agree with how the Republican party set up the tax system. You may like some aspects of it but not others. You may love all of it or hate all of it. The important thing is that you understand that the new Republican tax code is not distinct from the economy, it essentially *is* the economy (meaning the system of how the resources of our nation are divided up). And that economy affects your life and everyone else's life in the entire country. You should ask yourself whether or not this is how you would set things up if you had as much power as all those politicians in Washington (and their campaign donors).

Now, to be clear, you could read this entire section, hate everything about the new Republican tax code, and still decide that the Democrats wouldn't do it any better. When it comes to taxes, a pox on both their houses is probably the most reasonable position to take.

Over the last few decades, control of the federal government has flipped back and forth between the parties, and over that same period, regardless of who was in charge, taxes for millionaires and corporations have mostly gone down. We see the results of those choices today in our broken society.

We have federal elections every two years, and state and local elections in between. If the American people are paying attention and don't allow themselves to get hoodwinked by clever politicians and their wealthy backers, they can have the kind of tax code they want, regardless of who's in charge.

## Why We Choose Taxes

No one likes to see that chunk of their paycheck disappear, but everyone knows that in order to have the kind of country we want, some of us have to pay taxes. Resources that could be used for private purposes are instead used for public purposes. Some money that might be used to buy a gold-plated living room, for example, could be used to fund a school or improve our highway system. Money that might be used to buy a private jet could be used to build better airports for everyone.

When everyone pays their fair share, we are all, rich and poor, better off. We can and should have spirited disagreements about the proper amount of government spending. We should consider whether or not there should be a maximum level of taxation and why. Regardless of the details, let's at least conclude that some taxes have to be paid by some people. That basic idea has held this country (and civilization as a whole) together through its entire history. From the pharaohs of ancient Egypt five thousand years ago taking a fraction of every grain harvest, to your W-2 form, there's an unbroken line of taxes paying for the things that keep a society together.

You do, of course, have a choice. If you want to live in a tax-free "paradise," there are any number of conflict-ridden third-world countries you could move to. Anti-tax zealot Grover Norquist, who requires every Republican lawmaker to take a "No new taxes, ever" pledge, once got into a spirited conversation with several members of the Patriotic Millionaires about the merits of the Somali tax code. Mr. Norquist didn't

"Are your taxes based on usable living space or actual square footage?"

seem to understand that the reasons people would rather live in the United States than Somalia have nothing to do with our geography or our weather and everything to do with the protection and services that come from our tax dollars at work. (Or maybe he does understand it, because despite the higher tax rates here in America, we don't see him living in a condo in Mogadishu.)

So, anyway, there are plenty of arguments to be had about what we should and should not spend money on. Educate our children? Build a Space Force? Actually recycle? Find Bigfoot? We expect those fights to continue until the second-to-last person on earth takes their second-to-last-breath. But for this book's purposes, we are not concerned with the total amount of taxes. We're concerned with how they're divided up.

Before we jump in, let me briefly reference two kinds of taxes that are important but that we won't focus on in this book: taxes on goods and services (basically, sales taxes) and payroll taxes (taxes that come directly out of your paycheck to fund Social Security and Medicare).

## Taxes on Goods and Services

Your mom gives you a dollar for unloading the dishwasher, and you head straight for the candy store. You pick out a candy bar that costs exactly a dollar and plop it on the counter, only to find out that you can't afford that candy bar. Taxes. Sales tax, excise taxes (typically on something such as fuel), sin taxes (typically on cigarettes and alcohol), and user fees (think of the bill you get for a hotel room with all the additional taxes added)—these are all taxes on goods and services. These taxes are important, but they're largely imposed at the state and local level, so let's set them aside for a moment, as our focus is on understanding the major choices elected leaders have made in the federal tax system.

## Payroll Taxes

The next kind of taxes you become aware of are payroll taxes. Payroll taxes are called FICA taxes because they're authorized by the Federal Insurance Contributions Act. Think of them as your own sort of personal security taxes. Payroll taxes are the first way that you ensure you have an income and health care when you retire or become disabled and can't work. You contribute a little each month over the course of your entire working life so that when you can't work, you will be okay. FICA taxes are 7.65% of your salary, with 6.2% going to Social Security and the rest to Medicare. Employers match their employees' contributions, while self-employed people are required to contribute both the standard individual contribution and the employer match.

"Pay yourself first" is a common phrase in the world of personal-finance strategies. The goal is to ensure that you set aside money for savings or investments before you make other purchases. The idea is that you should pay yourself, meaning your future retired or disabled self (the one who will have to live on what your current self has managed to save after you can't work anymore), before you spend money on your current self—going to the movies or getting a new haircut. Payroll taxes are the way the government helps you do that.

Sidenote here: politicians periodically float the idea of a payroll-tax "holiday," because if that 7.65% isn't taken out of your paycheck and saved, you're likely to spend it buying things instead. When millions of people all do that at the same time, it stimulates the economy. The biggest problem with payroll tax holidays is that they allow your employer to skip out on matching your contribution to your future retirement. The second problem is that whenever FICA revenues go down, politicians use it as an excuse to start trying to cut Social Security and Medicare, which millions of people rely on and have been paying into their whole lives. When it comes to payroll tax holidays, just say no.

## Income Taxes

So you work, you make money, some of that money goes to payroll taxes (a.k.a. your personal security taxes), and then, depending on how much you make, you may have to kick some into the national kitty.

People don't pay income tax on the first chunk of their income. About 80% of taxpayers take what's called the standard deduction.[1] This refers to the first several thousand dollars of your income that is yours and yours alone, not subject to any income tax. Think of the standard deduction as the amount the government assumes you need all for yourself to cover your basic expenses. The government has decided that until you make more than this standard amount, you won't be

asked to contribute to all the stuff we need to get done together. As a reminder, you will be paying sales tax and various
other taxes into your local community, but let's keep it on the
federal level for now and say that as far as our national priorities are concerned, until you make above a certain amount, we
expect you to contribute to your local community, and possibly to your state, but not to the country's needs as a whole.

One of the best things about the new Republican tax code is
that it raised the standard deduction significantly. The deduction is adjusted a little bit each year, and it varies depending
on several additional factors, but let's keep it simple. In 2020,
for single people, the standard deduction was $12,400 and for
married people filing jointly it was $24,800. This means that
for a married couple, until you and your spouse have brought
home at least $24,800, you won't be asked to contribute any-
thing to the federal coffers. There are additional provisions
and endless important details, but for our purposes, we'll keep
it simple. After that point, the federal government will take a
little bit out of each dollar in income you earn to finance our
joint priorities. Here's where things start to get weird. Let the
rigging begin!

## Their Money vs. Your Sweat: A Case Study

*A quick note about the numbers in this section (and the rest of the book): Tax brackets change each year to account for inflation, so the amount of money being taxed at specific rates will change each year. The calculations below, and throughout the rest of this book, reflect the tax rates and tax brackets that were in effect in the year 2020 for married couples, unless otherwise indicated.*

Say that two people—we'll call them Doug and Carrie Werkhardt—both worked full-time last year, putting in forty hard hours every week. Together they made $100,000, just above average for a two-earner household. They subtract the $24,800 standard deduction and are left with $75,200 in taxable income. Under the new Republican tax code, the Werkhardts would pay around $8,629 in federal income taxes (in addition to FICA taxes of $7,650 on all their income, with 6.2% going to Social Security and 1.45% going to Medicare).

Now, say two other people—we'll call them Ronald and Melanie Slump—sat around all year playing golf and sipping strawberry daiquiris on a beach somewhere. One day, after reapplying sunscreen, Ronald clicked a button on the couple's E*TRADE account and sold some stock they've owned for a while. Let's say they made $100,000 in profit from the sale of that stock and lived off that all year. In our current tax plan, capital gains income is not subject to FICA taxes, so the Slumps would take the standard deduction of $24,800 and be left with $75,200 of taxable income, just like the Werkhardts.

The Slumps should pay around the same amount as the Werkhardts, right? Wrong. Under our current tax system, the Slumps will pay $0 in taxes on that income. Our tax system does not tax the first $80,000 of investment income (after deductions), but it does tax the first $80,000 of ordinary income (after deductions). The Werkhardts worked hard all year trying to get rich while the Slumps, who are already rich, sat on the beach sipping strawberry daiquiris. Yet at the end of that year, the Slumps are $8,629 richer ($16,279 if you count FICA taxes) than the Werkhardts. Pause here for a minute and consider whether or not that seems fair to you. One couple worked, the other couple got drunk on the beach. The drunk people end the year richer than the working people. Do you think the difference in our tax treatment of their money serves a legitimate purpose in our society?

Let's take it a little further. Let's say the Slumps switched to mai tais, and rather than making $100,000 in profit selling their stock, they sell enough to make $400,000 (it was a heavy pour). The Slumps will again take the $24,800 standard deduction and be left with $375,200 of taxable income. They will again pay 0% tax on the first $80,000 and will pay 15% on the remaining $295,200 for a total tax bill of around $44,280.

The Werkhardts also had a good year. They got new jobs, with two weeks of paid vacation (!), and made a total of $400,000 ($200,000 each) working forty hours a week for fifty weeks. They will pay FICA taxes of around $22,875 total. Like the Slumps, they took their $24,800 standard deduction and were left with taxable income of $375,200. But unlike the

*Depicts federal income tax bill.*

Slumps, they will pay 10% on the first $19,750; 12% on the next $60,500; 22% on the next $90,800; 24% on the next $155,500; and 32% on the remaining roughly $48,600 for a total tax bill of about $82,095 in income taxes plus $22,875 in FICA taxes, or $104,970 all together.

Two families make exactly the same amount of money, one by working full-time, the other by sipping cocktails and pushing a button on an E*TRADE account. The cocktail sippers end the year over $60,000 richer than the working people. Why?

Well, the tax code treats income differently depending on how you make it. There is one set of rates for money you get from a job (ordinary income) and another set of rates for money you make on long-term investments, such as stocks (capital gains), an option available only to people who already have enough money to be able to invest it.

- Ordinary income: The tax most people pay on their earnings, the ordinary income tax, is taken from money earned through labor. You go to work, receive a paycheck, and pay income tax (normally with some deducted from every paycheck).
- Capital gains income: The capital gains tax, on the other hand, is the rate paid on profit that comes from the sale of an asset, or a valuable thing that someone owns. You buy a stock or a piece of real estate, it goes up in value, and you sell it for a profit. That profit is considered a capital gain, and as long as you hold on to that asset for at least a year before selling it, you pay the much lower capital gains rate instead of

the ordinary income tax rate. (If you sell an asset less than a year after you acquire it, the profit from the sale is taxed at ordinary income tax rates.) Investors are supposed to figure out how much they think they should pay and send in checks four times per year.

Our elected officials may talk endlessly about the value of a hard day's work and the nobility of labor, but our tax code is deliberately designed to reward capital income over labor income. If you work for a living, you should understand this one thing about the tax code: a dollar made off a rich investor's money is worth more than a dollar made off your sweat. Think about that for a minute. If you are working, you keep less of every dollar you make compared with someone who is not working, who is living off their investments. If you think that's okay, then okay. But if you don't, you should talk with your elected leaders about it, whatever party they happen to be a member of.

There is no valid reason why investors should pay lower tax rates on their income than people who work pay on theirs. I often hear the argument that investors need an extra incentive to invest and the tax break provides that, but investors already have all the incentive they need to invest; here's why:

If I have $1 million and am thinking about what to do, I could (to simplify):

A. Keep my million dollars in cash. At the end of the year, I will still have $1 million, and I will owe no taxes at all.
B. Invest my $1 million, make additional money, and pay

taxes on whatever I made (whatever the rate may be). Even taking the volatility of the market into consideration, I'm extremely likely to make a significant amount of money from my investment. A higher tax rate may mean I don't make quite as much, but it's still better than making nothing!

The only logical choice is B!

I remember a conversation several members of the Patriotic Millionaires had with a junior staff person in the office of a Republican congressperson, when we want to contest the idea of preferential tax treatment for capital gains income over ordinary income. The staffer, who couldn't have been more than twenty-five years old, was trying to convince a room full of wealthy old investors that we wouldn't invest our money if his boss raised the tax rate on our investment income. He was so sure he was right. He actually became quite heated in his defense of our unfair tax advantage, and yet we were the investors! That's how things work in Washington—twenty-five-year-old staff people on government salaries passionately protecting millionaires' tax breaks.

The only tax-related reason not to invest would be if I were just so morally opposed to paying taxes that I would rather have no profit—and therefore no taxes—than have some taxes and more profit. We certainly don't want to discourage people from investing, but rich people are going to invest their money regardless of the tax rate. They are not going to keep their money in cash under their beds; we can promise you that.

| Long-Term Capital Gains Tax Rate | Single Taxpayers | Married Taxpayers Filing Together |
|---|---|---|
| 0% | Up to $40,000 | Up to $80,000 |
| 15% | $40,001 to $441,450 | $80,001 to $496,600 |
| 20% | $441,451 or more | $496,601 or more |

| Marginal Income Tax Rate | Single Taxpayers | Married Taxpayers Filing Together |
|---|---|---|
| 10% | Up to $9,875 | Up to $19,750 |
| 12% | $9,876 to $40,125 | $19,751 to $80,250 |
| 22% | $40,126 to $85,525 | $80,251 to $171,050 |
| 24% | $85,526 to $163,300 | $171,051 to $326,600 |
| 32% | $163,301 to $207,350 | $326,601 to $414,700 |
| 35% | $207,351 to $518,400 | $414,701 to $622,050 |
| 37% | $518,401 or more | $622,051 or more |

## It's a Rich Person's World

These two different forms of taxes are a big reason rich people just keep getting richer than everyone else. Really rich people in America, especially billionaires, don't earn much ordinary income. Most of the ultrarich make the vast majority of their money through capital gains on investments. And because the top tax rate they pay on each of their additional dollars is 20%, while the top rate for regular, earned income is 37%, no matter how much money a person makes by working, someone who makes their money by not working will always end up richer.

Only a very small number of households in the country report any capital gains income at all (about 6% of households in the bottom 80% of income earners).[2] But a whopping 83% of extremely rich people make at least some "lazy" money without working. On the whole, the top 1% earn more of their money through investments (41%) than through income (34%), and that ratio is even greater for the top 0.1% and the top 0.01%.[3] (In 2019, the top 1% of households accounted for 75% of all capital gains in the United States. The top 0.1%, a group of just a couple hundred thousand people making more than $3.8 million a year, earned nearly half of all capital gains income in the United States that year.)[4]

Rich people don't work the way most Americans work, exchanging labor for money. Instead, they live off of their investments; sometimes they make their investing decisions themselves, but more often they offload even this "work" to other people. And thanks to our tax code they basically get a "50% off" coupon.

## Rich People Earn a Much Higher Percentage of Their Income from Capital Gains Than the Rest of Us

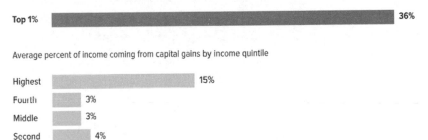

Percentage of income coming from capital gains

| | |
|---|---|
| Top 1% | 36% |

Average percent of income coming from capital gains by income quintile

| | |
|---|---|
| Highest | 15% |
| Fourth | 3% |
| Middle | 3% |
| Second | 4% |
| Lowest | 5% |

SOURCE: CONGRESSIONAL BUDGET OFFICE

## Most Capital Gains Are Earned by the Rich
Share of total capital gains, 2018

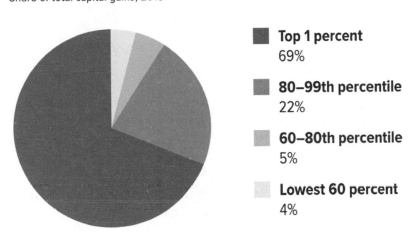

**Top 1 percent**
69%

**80–99th percentile**
22%

**60–80th percentile**
5%

**Lowest 60 percent**
4%

SOURCE: URBAN-BROOKINGS TAX POLICY CENTER, T18-0231

*Patriotic Millionaire Michael Lambert, former boat builder, married into wealth*

When I received our first joint tax return after marrying into a wealthy family, I was amazed that our effective tax rate was about half of what I was used to as a boat builder and arborist. And when one considers that I now didn't have to lift a finger to make more than I could have imagined, much less drag branches to the chipper in the hot sun, the injustice was palpable. I actually called our financial adviser to complain that I wasn't paying enough in taxes; she was confused, to say the least.

That brings me to another point: being rich has almost nothing to do with how much income you have. People (with rare exceptions) do not become rich by making a lot of money. People become rich by owning something that is or becomes very valuable. Someone once argued with me that I was wrong to call Jeff Bezos rich because he has a salary of only $80,000. That is true, but he also owns over 10% of Amazon and has sold hundreds of millions of dollars' worth of stock over the years.[5] To suggest that his salary has anything to do with his wealth or whether or not he is rich is absurd.

All the wealthiest people are wealthy because they own parts of valuable companies. Some of them, such as Mr. Bezos, founded their companies (Zuckerberg, Gates, Brin), and some greatly increased the value of companies that have been around for many years (Buffett, Arnault). Others were born into their wealth, but it is still based on owning something (Walton heirs, Mars heirs, Carlos Slim heirs, etc.).

Even the people who founded companies are wealthy mostly as a return on the investment they made in the early days of their company, not as a direct result of their labor at the time. Bill Gates became rich because he founded Microsoft, but he didn't become ridiculously rich while he was actively managing and adding value to the company; nearly half his wealth was actually created after he retired from Microsoft.

This is the secret to wealth that every rich person in America knows: working doesn't make you rich, making your money work for you does. But how are you ever going to make enough money to make your money work for you if you are paying twice the tax rate of the people who already have money? How will the Werkhardts ever have as much money as the Slumps if each and every year they pay a bigger percentage of their ordinary income in taxes than the Slumps pay from their investment income? It's simple; they won't.

# Tax Tricks (by Morris)

*The nation should have a tax system that looks like someone designed it on purpose.*
—William E. Simon , former U.S. Secretary
of the Treasury

Okay, we've concluded that working is a sucker's game; it's much better to already be rich and live off your investments. The difference in tax rates between ordinary income and investment/capital gains income comes from a long human tradition of valuing capital over labor, a tradition that is rotten to the core. Think of it as the "original sin" of the tax code. But it is far from the only trick. The ways rich people have found to hide their money are mind-blowing. Let's look at a few of the biggest sleights of hand rich people have snuck into our tax code.

## Trick #1: Carried Interest: "The Billionaires' Loophole"

Remember our earlier discussion about the justification for the difference in the tax rates between ordinary income and long-term capital gains income? Politicians and the millionaires who fund their campaigns insist that their investments need a preferential tax rate, lest all the millionaires and billionaires across the country stuff their money into giant mattresses and refuse to invest. As we noted, the preferential treatment is not particularly logical, given that if people don't invest their money, they will make no additional money, and anyone would rather make more money that will be taxed than make no money that won't be taxed. But be that as it may, as it now stands, if you invest your own capital, you will pay lower taxes on the money you make than if you had worked for it.

Now, you may ask yourself, is there any way to get the preferential investment income tax rate without actually having to invest your own capital? As luck would have it, yes! We'll look to billionaire investor David Rubenstein to show us how to do it.

Rubenstein is the founder of the Carlyle Group, a private-equity firm based on the idea of "access capitalism" (his words, not ours). Rubenstein is well known for his "patriotic philanthropy," where he spends generously (and very publicly) on "giving back to the nation." When an earthquake shook the foundation of the Washington Monument, for example, he put up several million dollars to help with the repair.[1]

What many of the glowing profiles of Rubenstein fail to

mention is that he earned a significant chunk of his billions because of the carried-interest loophole—the poster child for the rigged economy and the corrupting influence of money on tax policy.[2]

The carried-interest loophole allows fund managers—people who invest *other* people's money (not their own money)—to mischaracterize their ordinary income as capital gains income. By pretending they are partners with their wealthy investors, fund managers claim that their earnings are long-term capital gains. Because their investors are investing for the long term, and because they are partners, they say, they deserve their so-called partners' tax benefits. This lets some of the richest people in the country cut their personal tax bills nearly in half by using the much lower capital gains tax rate of 20% rather than the top income tax rate of 37%, despite having none of their own capital at risk.

The term *carried interest* goes back to the medieval merchants in Genoa, Pisa, Florence, and Venice, Italy. These traders carried cargo on their ships belonging to other people and earned 20% of the profits on the "carried" product.[3] At the time, this made sense because the shipmen had to risk storms, sickness, and pirates to ensure the product made it to port. The people who receive carried interest today lead much more comfortable lives (to say the least) and certainly don't need any additional tax incentive to participate in an industry as lucrative as private equity fund management.

There are only a few thousand fund managers in the United States who benefit from carried interest, and by mischaracterizing their income, each member of this small group of fund managers earns somewhere in the realm of an extra $300,000 a year on average *just in tax savings*! They already earn millions of dollars a year, yet they pay a lower tax rate than any working person in America does because the tax code gives them a way to legally lie about how they make their income.

Remember, we are talking about fund managers who invest *other people's* money. They take no risk of their own; they are simply managing the investment funds of other rich people. Here's how it works.

## Two and Twenty

Private-equity firms collect money from a group of wealthy people and then manage that money for them by investing in private companies or buying out public ones. In return for the firms' work, they're paid a fee by their investors.

The typical fee structure for a private-equity or hedge fund is something called "two and twenty"; fund managers are paid 2% of the total value of the assets they manage every year and then 20% of the fund's profits above a certain threshold as an incentive for them to do well. For example, if a fund manager is managing $1 billion, his 2% takeaway fee is $20 million, which he receives no matter how well or poorly the fund does. If he makes a profit of $200 million above the required threshold, then he will also take away 20% of that profit, or an additional $40 million, so his total income for the year will be $60 million.

Of this income, the $20 million will be taxed at normal income tax rates, but the $40 million "carry" will be considered capital gains and taxed at those lower rates. Why? Well, because according to the fund managers, they are partners with the investors. The investors are investing the capital, and the managers are investing their time and expertise. The managers earn nothing (except for their $20 million fee), they argue, if the fund doesn't make a profit. Shouldn't that count as investment and risk and qualify their earnings as capital gains?

No. It shouldn't. The investment of time and expertise in exchange for money is literally the definition of employment. Millions of people in thousands of industries get bonuses for performance, and virtually all those bonuses are taxed as ordinary income. Why should carried interest be any different? When a car salesman earns a commission for selling cars, that's considered ordinary income. The salesman is managing the sale of the dealership's cars—someone else's capital investments—but because he's operating out of a suburban car lot instead of a high-rise in Manhattan, his earnings face the standard tax rate.

Keeping the loophole open doesn't help investors, because investors already get the preferential capital gains rate. Closing this loophole would affect only the fund managers' tax rate on the fees they earn, for the pay they receive for simply doing their job.

This particular loophole is protected by a huge amount of money. When our organization tried to close the carried-interest loophole on a state level in California, every single venture-capital fund in the state signed a letter claiming that closing a loophole that benefits a few thousand fund managers would crash the state's economy, cause investors to flee to other states, upend decades of partnership law, blah-blah-blah. Chicken Little would have been proud of this letter. No one who signed it should be.

The carried-interest loophole is a litmus test for politicians, but it's also a litmus test for the money people on both sides of the political aisle. It's an easy way to separate real patriots from people who like to get their picture taken with politicians and be lauded for their "patriotism" while, behind the scenes, they sell out the country.

## They All Think They Deserve Special Treatment

### by Erica

It's kind of amazing to me how persistent the carried interest loophole is. A while back, the *New Yorker* published a long article about David Rubenstein's multi-decade fight to defend this loophole. The article questioned whether the patriotic philanthropy this loophole facilitated justified its continued existence. The answer is, Of course not. But Rubenstein isn't the only billionaire who loves this loophole.

A couple of years ago, a different billionaire called me out of the blue to say that he was intrigued by the Patriotic Millionaires and wanted to learn more. We spoke for about forty-five minutes, and through most of the conversation, he was quite enthusiastic about our work. But then we got to the carried-interest loophole. I explained how important I thought this loophole was on a basic fairness level and explored some of the ways we had attacked this tax injustice. He interrupted me rather sternly and then proceeded to mansplain to me for several minutes why every industry deserves its little benefits in the tax code, so I really shouldn't spend so much time on this one. This billionaire, who is a top (Democratic) political donor, just couldn't stand the idea of giving up his special little perk—and he sure as heck wasn't going to join a group of millionaires working to get rid of his special loophole, no matter how unfair it was.

All these billionaires are fighting for their special piece of the pie, trying to convince the public that they are good people and hoping no one notices the money they are tucking into their pockets on the sly. Needless to say, the mansplaining billionaire declined to join our little group.

"OUR GOAL IS TO ELIMINATE TAX LOOPHOLES... SO FROM NOW ON THEY'LL BE CALLED DONUT HOLES."

# Trick #2: The Estate Tax: How We Created an American Aristocracy

For a long time, I was under the impression that we fought a war against England and started our own country because we wanted things here to be different, but take a deep dive into our tax code and you may find yourself humming "God Save the Queen." We say we want liberty and justice for all, but our tax system clearly prefers an aristocracy.

When most Americans think of the rich, they think of people who have been successful and worked hard to earn their money. But that's not how wealth in America actually works. Between 35% to 45% of all wealth in America is inherited.[4] Many of the richest people in America aren't rich because they did something to earn it; they're rich because their parents or grandparents (or their parents' grandparents) did something to earn it. There's nothing wrong with inheriting money, of course. Parents and grandparents naturally want to provide for their families. But there's no particularly good reason that inheritance income should be taxed differently from other kinds of income.

Let's go back and check in with the Werkhardts and the Slumps. When we last left them, the Werkhardts were working their tails off and the Slumps were drunk on the beach. Well, as luck would have it, the Werkhardts are very good singers. Last year they quit their jobs and started singing full-time for a great company called America Sings. They are such good singers that last year America Sings paid the two of them

$22 million. The Werkhardts subtracted the $25,000 standard deduction and were left with $21,975,0000 of ordinary income. They paid 10% on the first $20,000, 12% on the next $50,000, 22% on the next roughly $90,000, and so forth, finally maxing out at 37% for all the income over $600,000. Their total tax bill for the year was around $8 million.

The Slumps also had a very good year (hangovers and skin-cancer scare notwithstanding). Mr. Slump's great aunt and uncle died and left him their entire $22 million estate. (Don't worry, they were very old and they weren't close.) The Slumps heard the news while having Sex on the Beach (the drink, of course, what kind of book do you think this is?!) and immediately called their accountant to ask how much money they would owe in taxes on their inheritance income of $22 million. Their accountant explained that they would owe $0 in taxes. Mr. Slump passed out from the shock (or possibly the drinks) and had to confirm the information the next day, but, yes, it was true. Neither the aunt nor the uncle nor their estate nor the Slumps would pay any taxes at all on the $22 million.

Once again, the Werkhardts and the Slumps took in exactly the same amount of *pre-tax income*, but because they earned their money in different ways, one couple by working and the other by waiting for people to die, the Slumps ended the year $8 million richer than the Werkhardts. Once again, the Werkhardts worked very hard, and the Slumps didn't work at all. But the Slumps came out ahead because they inherited their money.

"*Sure I play hard, but I also inherit hard.*"

## Plutocracy Prevention: Our First Line of Defense
## Against Concentrations of Wealth and Power

An intergenerational wealth transfer tax is the best way for a country to prevent wealth and power from getting concentrated in the hands of a few unproductive families. Not having a meaningful intergenerational wealth transfer tax (an estate or inheritance tax) has allowed a form of aristocracy—a nonworking, wealthy class of people—to develop in America, people my grandmother would have called "rich bums."

The new Republican tax code exempts the first $11.58 million of an estate from the estate tax. A married couple can combine their two exemptions, allowing them to pass on $23.16 million tax free. Above that amount, the estate pays a 40% tax. For example, if your parents leave an estate of

Intergenerational wealth transfer taxes can be structured in a few ways. The United States' intergenerational wealth transfer tax is currently structured as an estate tax, meaning that the estate of the deceased pays the tax prior to transferring the inheritance income to the recipient. This structure has allowed opponents (mostly wealthy heirs) to label it a "death tax" (they bemoan how cruel we are to take someone's money when they are no longer in a position to defend themselves!) and build support against it. Eliminating the estate tax and instead implementing an inheritance tax , which taxes the person inheriting the money instead of the deceased person's estate, would likely aid efforts to build support for taxing the intergenerational transfer of wealth. At a minimum, intergenerational wealth transfers should be taxed at ordinary income levels.

$24.16 million, their estate (and by extension you, their heir) would pay tax on only the $1 million above the exemption. On an inheritance of $24.16 million, one million dollars over the exemption limit, you would pay around $400,000 in estate taxes. On an inheritance of $23,160,001, one dollar over the exemption limit, you would owe less than 40¢.

We haven't always given such massive tax discounts to inheritance income. The exemption threshold, or the point at which people have to start paying the tax, used to be much lower. In 2001, the exemption was just $675,000 per person. It slowly grew from there. In 2017, when the Republicans rewrote the federal tax code, they doubled the threshold from $5.59 million to $11.2 million per person ($22.4 million per couple).[5]

Republicans call the estate tax the death tax because it sounds scary. But in some ways, the estate tax is the least scary tax there is because, by definition, it only kicks in once you are no longer around to notice it.

The estate tax is really important because it is often the *only* tax levied on the transfer of wealth from one generation to the next. When we set the tax rate, we are making a value judgment about how much free money some genetically-lucky person should be able to get in a country that was founded on the idea of equality among people. To restate the obvious (because lots of people have been deliberately misled by anti-taxers on this point): intergenerational wealth transfer taxes, however they are structured, apply only to extremely wealthy families.

Continuing to raise the taxable threshold doesn't help

# The Estate Tax Exemption Threshold Has Risen Dramatically Since 2001

| Year | Per-Person Exemption | Top Rate |
|------|----------------------|----------|
| 2001 | $675,000 | 55% |
| 2002 | $1 million | 50% |
| 2003 | $1 million | 49% |
| 2004 | $1.5 million | 48% |
| 2005 | $1.5 million | 47% |
| 2006 | $2 million | 46% |
| 2007 | $2 million | 45% |
| 2008 | $2 million | 45% |
| 2009 | $3.5 million | 45% |
| 2010 | None | 0% |
| 2011 | $5 million | 35% |
| 2012 | $5.1 million | 35% |
| 2013 | $5.25 million | 40% |
| 2014 | $5.34 million | 40% |
| 2015 | $5.43 million | 40% |
| 2016 | $5.45 million | 40% |
| 2017 | $5.49 million | 40% |
| 2018 | $11.18 million | 40% |
| 2019 | $11.4 million | 40% |
| 2020 | $11.58 million | 40% |

Source: Internal Revenue Service

middle-class Americans or create jobs or boost the economy. It does nothing more than give more money to the children of the rich, who did literally nothing to earn that money (except possibly suck up to their parents).

Many of the wealthiest people in the country believe we should only tax people who work for their income—and that the children of the rich, who inherit money and who have never worked a day in their life, should not pay any taxes. I believe that at a minimum, money earned from working should be treated in the same way as money earned in easier ways, such as by selling stocks or inheriting from parents.

## Only 1.4 Out of Every 1,000 Estates in the United States Owed Any Estate Taxes in 2013

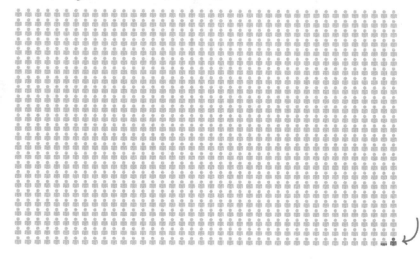

SOURCE: TAX POLICY CENTER

## A Word About the Family Farm

During the debate over the Republican tax bill, Republican Representative Kristi Noem, who is now governor of South Dakota, told the tragic story of how, after her father's accidental death, her family was hounded by the IRS for the government's cut of his estate. She claimed that in their time of tragedy, her family was forced to either sell the land that had been in their family for generations or take out a loan to pay off the estate tax, which is what they ended up doing.[6]

It's a sad story. Or rather it would be one, if it were typical, or happening at all under the current tax code. After some digging, journalists found that things didn't add up. The story was more complicated than Noem told it, and the tax due could have been completely avoided had her father left the farm in his will to her mother.[7]

As it turns out, almost no small businesses or family farms are worth enough to qualify for the estate tax at all. In 2017, the owners of only about fifty small farms or businesses *in the entire United States* owed any estate tax at all, and since the Trump tax bill increased how much money you need to inherit to be forced to pay any estate tax, that number is likely even lower in recent years. Those who did owe taxes paid, on average, less than 6% of their total value in estate tax. So the owners of fifty small farms and businesses had to pay a 6% tax after inheriting millions worth of money and assets.[8] That hardly seems like an insidious plot to destroy the family farm.

## Trick #3: Sidestepping Taxes: The Stepped-Up Basis

At this point, you may be thinking to yourself, Well, $23.16 million is not what it used to be, and these poor grief-stricken heirs are at least paying some taxes on some of their inheritance income, even if it's only the amount above the threshold. Okay.

But thanks to a loophole called the stepped-up basis, the person who inherits will likely never pay taxes on the vast majority of the value of their inheritance, regardless of how much that inheritance is. Here's how they do it.

The stepped-up basis is a tax benefit for people inheriting assets such as stocks, houses, or land instead of money. Keep in mind, the ultrarich do not keep their fortunes in cash. Families such as the Waltons who own Walmart are worth tens of billions of dollars, yet when they sell some of their stock to make money to live on, they do not pay any tax on most of their profits. That is because of the stepped-up basis.

Here's how it works. Think back to our discussion of capital gains taxes. You sell an asset such as a stock, and you pay taxes on the difference between what you bought it for and what you sold it for. You get taxed on the profit, or the gain on the capital. The price you bought the stock at is considered the "basis," meaning it is the basis against which you figure out how much your gain was. If you bought a stock for $10 and sold it for $12, your basis is $10 and your gain is $2, and you're taxed only on that $2.

If you bought a bundle of stocks worth $10 million a few

years ago and then sold it today for $100 million, you would have to pay taxes on the difference, on the "capital gain" of $90 million. The basis, or starting price, is subtracted from the sale price to calculate your profit from the sale, and then, at the time of the sale, you pay capital gains taxes only on that profit.

But you pay capital gains taxes only when you actually sell the assets, not when their value goes up. What happens if you don't sell those stocks? They could go up forever and you would never pay taxes on them; because if you don't sell the stocks, you haven't "realized" the gain. You don't pay taxes on the increased value, because you haven't "realized" it yet. There's an argument to be made that people should not be able to wait to pay taxes on capital gains until they sell their assets (see the section on Mark-to-Market taxation in Chapter 7), but that's how things work right now. Your assets can get more and more valuable, and you never have to pay a cent on them until you sell them.

Some of the richest families in America have huge amounts of assets that have never been and will never be taxed. Sam Walton, the founder of Walmart, avoided paying taxes on almost all the increased value of his ownership stake in the company, which went from zero to tens of billions of dollars over his lifetime. When a significant portion of that stake was passed on to his family after he died, that increase in capital gains value was largely eliminated through the stepped-up basis as far as the IRS was concerned. Now his three living children, who collectively own about half of all Walmart stock, are among the twenty richest people on the planet.

Now, let's say several years ago you bought some stock for $10 million, you never sold any of it, and it grew to be worth $100 million. But the day before you planned to sell the stock, you die. What would happen then? Well, what *should* happen is that your estate would be settled, the estate taxes would be paid, your stock would be passed on to your heirs, and then when they sold it, they would have to pay taxes on all the increased value that accumulated during your life.

Shockingly, that is not what happens. Under the stepped-up basis—a loophole specifically designed to facilitate huge intergenerational transfers of wealth—something special happens to your stock when it is transferred to your heirs. Poof! The basis of that stock magically changes. Instead of the basis being the value of that stock when you originally bought it ($10 million), the basis is adjusted to the value of the stock at the time of your death, when it is transferred to your heirs ($100 million). The value is "stepped-up" to a new basis, and—voilà!—no capital gain.

Your estate will pay the estate tax, but neither you nor your heirs would ever pay any tax on the capital gains. So if (after your estate pays the estate tax) your heirs inherit $100 million of investments with a previous basis of $10 million, when they eventually sell those investments they'll have to pay taxes only on any gains above the $100 million value it had when they inherited it. If they hold on to it and then sell it for $120 million a few years later, they'll be required to pay capital gains tax only on the $20 million in gains since they inherited it, not on the full $110 million increase in value it has accumulated since you originally bought it. All the increase in wealth during your lifetime—a full $90 million—is just wiped clean. It will never be taxed. Your family gets $90 million and doesn't pay a capital gains tax on that increase.

The total amount of tax being avoided through the stepped-up basis is staggering. According to the U.S. Treasury, taxing capital gains at death instead of allowing them to be passed on untaxed would raise over $400 billion for the country over the next decade, almost exclusively from the richest 1%.[9]

Dozens of wealthy families have benefited from the stepped-up basis. Many of these families have more money than they could ever reasonably spend, so there's no reason for them ever to sell the majority of their assets. They inherit them at a certain basis, hold on to them, watch them grow in value, and eventually pass the assets on to the next generation, at a new and greatly improved basis. Rinse and repeat. Along the way, the next generation can sell some or all of the assets, pay zero taxes, use as much of the money as they want to live on, and continue the cycle again.

The system is already stacked in their favor with capital gains being taxed at a lower rate than normal income, but the stepped-up basis rigs the system even further. No working family can beat that built-in advantage. The stepped-up basis is a shortcut to an American aristocracy: a permanently, hereditarily wealthy elite, the polar opposite of this country's founding ideals.

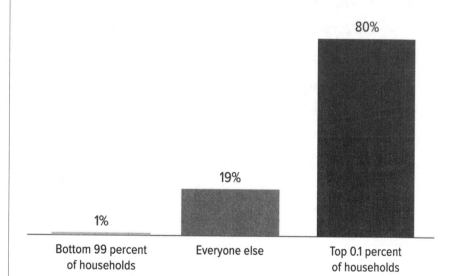

## The Stepped-Up Basis Is Almost Exclusively a Loophole for Rich Households

Percentage of revenue that abolishing the stepped-up basis would raise, by income group

80%

19%

1%

Bottom 99 percent
of households

Everyone else

Top 0.1 percent
of households

SOURCE: TAX POLICY CENTER

## Standing Up to the Stepped-Up Basis

This loophole is so obviously unfair that experts almost unanimously consider it one of the most regressive parts of the tax code, and support for closing it has come from unlikely places. Despite their embrace of low taxes for the rich, the stepped-up basis is a step too far for some Republicans. Senator Mitt Romney, a beneficiary of intergenerational wealth transfer, has partnered with Democratic Senator Michael Bennet to propose a bill to eliminate the stepped-up basis.[10] When even Mitt Romney, a multimillionaire supporter of the Tax Cuts and Jobs Act, thinks something is skewed too far in favor of the wealthy, it should be obvious that there's a problem.

## Trick #4: Annuity Trusts: Don't Trust This System

In theory, whatever the exemption threshold, the estate tax is supposed to tax the transfer of intergenerational wealth between family members. In reality, wealthy families use all manner of legal jujitsu to pass on billions of dollars to their heirs completely tax free, often while they're still alive. Enter the GRAT, or the grantor-retained annuity trust. Here's how it works.

A rich person puts some assets they own, such as stocks, into what's called a fixed-term, irrevocable trust (the GRAT). The trust invests their money for them and pays the rich person a set amount every year for a predetermined number of years. At the end of the GRAT's term, any remaining value is given to a beneficiary selected by the person who set up the

GRAT, often their children or grandchildren. If that amount were just given directly to the beneficiary, it would be subject to gift taxes. But by cycling it through a GRAT, it's allowed to pass on completely tax free.

Say you want to pass your wealth on to your daughter without paying taxes on it. You create a GRAT with her as the beneficiary. You put $50 million worth of stock in the trust, and the people in charge of the trust manage that investment. They guarantee an annual payment to you of $10 million every year for five years, no matter how much the value of that stock actually changes. After that five years is up, whatever is left goes to your daughter.

If the value of those stocks stays completely flat and doesn't change at all, she gets nothing, because the annual payments you receive will completely drain that $50 million. But if the collection of stocks rises in value, as assets chosen for GRATs tend to do, then she will receive what could end up being a sizable amount. If over those five years the value of the assets in your trust ended up increasing by 50%, the final value is $75 million. Because you only got back your initial investment of $50 million, the $25 million left over is given to your daughter, tax free.

The GRAT came about in 1990 (when Congress accidentally created the loophole while trying to close another one).[11] In the three decades since, this financial maneuver has become widespread in wealthy circles, to the point where it's almost bizarre to find a billionaire without any GRATs. Many rich people see them as so effective that paying estate tax is viewed more as a choice than an inevitability. Remember when Gary

Cohn, former chief White House economic adviser, said, "Only morons pay the estate tax"?[12] Well, the morons clearly don't know about GRATs.

Only a relatively small number of people have enough money to make a GRAT worthwhile, but the amount of money being passed through them is enormous. The man who invented the GRAT, tax lawyer Richard Covey, says that the loophole may have cost the federal government over $100 billion between 2000 and 2013 alone.

Sheldon Adelson, Las Vegas casino mogul and Republican mega-donor, is particularly fond of GRATs. Adelson, worth tens of billions of dollars, has created dozens of GRATs to pass along his substantial fortune while avoiding gift and estate taxes. As of 2013, he had used them to transfer nearly $8 billion to various members of his family, avoiding $2.8 billion in gift or estate taxes. Adelson isn't alone. President Trump inherited a significant part of his fortune from his father through GRATs, and Mark Zuckerberg, Ralph Lauren, and eighty-four current and former partners at Goldman Sachs have set up their own GRATs as well.

## Trick #5: Let's Play Switch and Swap: The 1031 Like-Kind Exchange

By now you have probably noticed that the tax code is full of little gimmicks most people have never heard of that allow small groups of people to make huge amounts of money. By some wild coincidence, the people who benefit from these tricks always end up being wealthy and politically influential. Who could have predicted that?

One deserves extra attention as it benefits a certain real-estate developer turned President of the United States. That's the 1031 exchange—also known as a like-kind exchange—which allows investors to avoid paying capital gains taxes when they sell buildings or other property. By using a 1031 exchange, real-estate owners can delay paying capital gains taxes on the sale of a property as long as the money from that sale is immediately invested into a similar property or properties.

Let's say a real-estate developer buys a building worth $10 million. He holds on to that building for a few years as real-estate prices in the area go up, then sells it for $35 million. But instead of keeping that money, he reinvests it in another building that he buys for $35 million. He sells that building a few years later for $60 million and buys another one for that price. The $60 million building then doubles in value over the next several years, leaving the developer with a building worth $120 million. Despite the gains of $110 million and two separate sales, the developer has paid no taxes.

And developers don't have to just trade their properties one for one. They can diversify their holdings by selling one expensive building and using the money from that sale to buy many cheaper buildings as well. So instead of selling a $60 million building and buying another one for the same price, a developer could use that $60 million to buy ten different $6 million buildings, and still pay no capital gains taxes.

Or buy one hundred different $600,000 buildings. Or one thousand $60,000 buildings. Still no capital gains taxes.

## When Loopholes Work Together

The worst part about the 1031 exchange is how it interacts with the stepped-up basis. Because the 1031 exchange allows people to defer paying capital gains taxes on the increased value of their property, and because the stepped-up basis resets the value of assets such as property when they are transferred to an heir after the original owner's death, real-estate families can acquire billions of dollars' worth of property without ever paying a cent in taxes.

Say someone starts off with $10 million. They buy and sell a series of properties, each time rolling their earnings over into buying a new property. At the end of their life, after estate taxes, they own $210 million worth of property. If that property gets passed down to their heirs, the new basis becomes $210 million. Their heirs would pay absolutely nothing in taxes if they sold it for $210 million, and if they sold it for more, they would have to pay taxes only on the profit over $210 million, rather than the entire profit from the original $10 million investment. These two loopholes added together allow wealthy real-estate developers and their families to amass incredible wealth without paying capital gains taxes.

# Trick #6: Help the Rich by Pretending to Help the Poor: Opportunity (for Rich People) Zones

The new Republican tax code doesn't just include obvious handouts to the rich—it also includes handouts to the rich disguised as help for the poor. Sold as a way to increase private investment in poor communities that might not otherwise be able to attract investors, Opportunity Zones are regions in which investors can avoid paying some of the normal taxes associated with real-estate and business investing. Opportunity Zones are a great idea in theory. In practice, though, not so much.

The implementation and selection of Opportunity Zones in the Tax Cuts and Jobs Act has done quite a lot to help wealthy real-estate investors and very little to help needy communities. Opportunity Zones offer an unprecedented amount of tax savings for wealthy people on at least two key forms of investment:

- *Past Investments In . . . Whatever:* An investor can avoid paying taxes on their profits from *any* past investment for up to seven years, as long as they invest an amount equal to those profits in an Opportunity Zone in the same year that they sell the investment. If you make $1 million in capital gains on the sale of your third home in the Hamptons, you can avoid paying any taxes on that money for seven years as long as you invest $1 million into an Opportunity Zone. Delaying tax payments is just as valuable as cutting them, because a dollar today that's invested can earn more than a dollar in the future.

"It was an artist's loft. Now it's a lawyer's loft."

- *Long-Term Investments in Opportunity (for Rich People) Zones*: Once investors own a piece of property within an Opportunity Zone, all they need to do is be patient. As long as they hold the property for at least ten years, they will pay zero taxes on the profits from their investment.

These two tax breaks add up to a colossal loophole. Investors can both delay paying taxes on old investments for years, and completely avoid *ever* paying taxes on profits from their new investments in Opportunity Zones.

All this would be somewhat more forgivable if the Opportunity Zones were actually helping low-income communities grow and prosper. But many of the Opportunity Zones aren't actually the kind of low-income areas that need help attracting investors. They may have been poor several years ago, but the rapid pace of gentrification in many of the country's largest cities has led to many Opportunity Zones being situated in areas such as the Warehouse District in New Orleans, Miami's Design District, and the Far West Side of Manhattan, each of which are actually already well-off.

Rather than incentivizing new growth in low-income areas, many Opportunity Zones just give developers a tax break for projects such as luxury condos and expensive hotels that they would have built anyway. According to a *New York Times* exposé on Opportunity Zone investment, "Even supporters of the initiative agree that the bulk of the opportunity-zone money is going to places that do not need the help."[13]

## The Opportunity Zone Loophole at Work

It's hard to overstate just how significant this is. Say you invested $1,000 in some Apple stock in 1982. That investment today would be worth about $1,000,000. If you sold that investment, you would have to pay a long-term capital gains tax of about $170,000 on a profit of $999,000.

But what if instead of selling the stock and pocketing the cash, you reinvest that money in a luxury apartment building in Long Island City, an Opportunity Zone and rapidly gentrifying neighborhood in Queens? You'd have to pay that $170,000 at some point in the next seven years, but by delaying that payment, you could invest the full $1 million right away (if you couldn't defer payment on your initial investment, you would only be able to invest $830,000 to start out).

Then say you hold on to that apartment building for ten years, and it goes up in value by 5% per year (after expenses). At the end of the ten years, your investment in the building would be worth about $1.6 million. You could then sell it and pay zero taxes on the extra $600,000 you made, giving you a total tax bill of $170,000 on $1.6 million in earnings. You would end up with about $1,430,000—one-third of a million dollars more than if you had invested that money in a normal property without preferential tax treatment, in which case you would have ended up earning about $1,100,000 instead.

# Trick #7: Just Passing Through: The Pass-Through Deduction

Politicians love talking about how great their tax policies are for small businesses. Republicans like small business so much that in their new tax code, they invented a way for rich people to pretend to be small businesses without actually having to do any "business" at all. Pass-throughs are a category of legal entities—including partnerships, S corporations, limited-liability companies (LLCs), and sole proprietorships—that make up the majority of businesses in America. While most large, publicly owned companies, such as Disney or Walmart or Amazon, are classified as C corporations (businesses that are taxed separately from their owners and are subject to the corporate income tax rate), the profits from smaller businesses, or pass-throughs, are taxed as personal income for their owners and come with amazing benefits: In their rewrite of the federal tax code, Republican provided a 20% deduction for pass-through income, meaning pass-through owners can take 20% off their income and not pay taxes on it. For example, on $100,000 in profit that the owner of a local plumbing company brought in, he would be able to subtract $20,000 from his total taxable income, meaning he would have to pay taxes as if his shop earned only $80,000 that year. "Pass-throughs," whose name comes from the concept of earnings "passing through" the business to the owner, currently account for nineteen out of every twenty businesses in the United States.[14]

The pass-through deduction was sold as something that would help businesses and workers alike. And by helping

Much like squares and rectangles, almost every small business is a pass-through, but not every pass-through is a small business. In fact, according to data from the Department of the Treasury, less than half of all people who claim pass-through income conduct any actual business activity, and of those who do, the majority are self-employed, with no additional employees. Of all the people claiming pass-through income, only about 10% are actually small businesses with employees (such as a dentist with a receptionist, for example).[17]

small businesses, its supporters claimed, it would help grow the economy, increase wages, and create jobs. But once again, something that seems like a good idea on the surface just turns out to be another way for rich people to game the system.

The classic image of a small-business owner in the American mind might be that of a hardworking middle-class person—a local dry cleaner or hardware-store owner, for example. But generally speaking, middle-class people just don't make much pass-through income. Most middle-class people work for someone else, and funneling employment income through a pass-through requires jumping through too many legal hoops, and disqualifying yourself for benefits such as health insurance, for it to be worth it.

The middle 60% of income earners in America earned an average of just 6% of their income from pass-throughs, compared to nearly one-fifth of the income of the top 1%.[15] Because of this split, most pass-through income goes to the rich: 85% of pass-through income goes to the top 20% of taxpayers, and more than 50% goes to the top 1%.

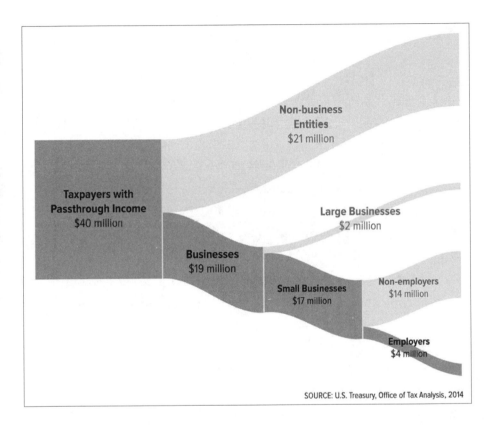

Non-business
Entities
$21 million

Taxpayers with
Passthrough Income
$40 million

Large Businesses
$2 million

Businesses
$19 million

Small Businesses
$17 million

Non-employers
$14 million

Employers
$4 million

SOURCE: U.S. Treasury, Office of Tax Analysis, 2014

This tax break is predicted to cost the country more than $50 billion per year, eventually making up over a fifth of the total cost of the Republican tax bill.

More egregious still, most pass-throughs owned by rich people aren't actual businesses at all. They're just pieces of paper that say a business exists and therefore this person should get to deduct 20% of their income when calculating their taxes. The requirements for classifying yourself and your income as a pass-through are incredibly lenient, making this process a simple one. A National Bureau of Economic Research paper suggests that nearly 75% of all pass-through income is really just normal personal income funneled through a shell business.[16] It's easy for any rich person with the resources to hire a competent tax lawyer to turn almost all their income into pass-through income, giving them a 20% cut on their taxable income.

This kind of financial maneuvering is out of reach for most Americans, but for those making millions of dollars a year, it's relatively simple. It's particularly easy for wealthy people with many forms of income that aren't necessarily tied to employment, but it's possible even for those working for another business. All they have to do is set up a pass-through in their name, be reclassified as an "independent contractor" instead of an employee by their employer, and then their salary is taxed as money paid between two companies instead of as the normal income that a person working in a job would receive.

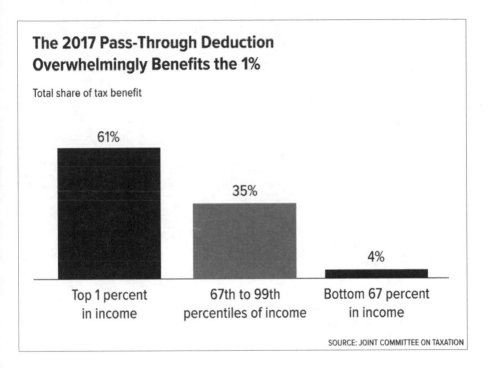

**The 2017 Pass-Through Deduction Overwhelmingly Benefits the 1%**

Total share of tax benefit

61% — Top 1 percent in income

35% — 67th to 99th percentiles of income

4% — Bottom 67 percent in income

SOURCE: JOINT COMMITTEE ON TAXATION

# The Double Irish Dutch Sandwich and Other Corporate Tax Machinations (by Morris)

Okay, so we have all these wealthy people pretending to be businesses so that they can avoid taxes. Well, what about real businesses. What are they doing about taxes?

The people who lead big U.S. and multinational corporations have been playing fast and loose with their responsibilities for so long now, it's hard to know where to even start trying to explain it all. But because this is a book about taxes, we might as well start there. Everyone has seen the headlines:

"[Insert company here] Paid $0 in Taxes Last Year!"

"You Paid More in Taxes Last Year Than This Billion-Dollar Company"

"New Study Shows That Dozens of Profitable Companies Paid No Taxes at All This Year"

Intellectually, I know how this happens. As an active

investor, I have an understanding of how companies structure various arrangements to avoid paying taxes on billions of dollars of profit. As a shareowner in big corporations, I often personally benefit from these arrangements, and yet I still periodically think to myself, How on earth is this possible?! I can only guess how it looks to the average observer.

The abuse is so rampant that the industry has all these clever little phrases for the various schemes corporations have used through the years to avoid taxes. One of my favorites is the Double Irish Dutch Sandwich, which sounds like something they would serve at Starbucks (which it kind of is; that particular coffee company sure does love an Irish tax break). The Double Irish Dutch Sandwich involves a company sending profits through an Irish company, and then along to a Dutch company, and from there back to another Irish company headquartered in a tax haven, all to get out of paying taxes. Google used that one for years, finally announcing at the end of 2019 that they would stop . . . after huge public outcry led Ireland to announce it was ending the loophole itself.[1]

CEOs just can't seem to help themselves. They can't seem to grasp that all the stakeholders, including the executives and the shareholders and society as a whole, will be better off if the management teams of our major businesses are thinking about the long term, rather than just the share price over the next three months. They justify all the bad choices they make with two little words: "shareholder value" (all due respect to the Business Roundtable's recently released "modern standard for corporate responsibility," of course). Let's start with understanding exactly how big the problem is.

In 2018, if you ordered a toothpick from Amazon, you paid more for your delivery than Amazon paid in federal income taxes for the entire year. If you watched a single movie on Netflix, you paid more for your subscription than Netflix paid in federal income taxes for all of 2018. If you filled up your car once, you paid more than Chevron paid in federal income taxes in 2018.

This is not an accident. Remember, the corporate tax code was written by people. If these corporations aren't paying any taxes, it's because the people who write the tax code decided to let some of the largest, most profitable companies in the world (along with their CEOs and shareholders) get away with contributing virtually nothing to our society. These companies are providing none of the money we need to pave the roads they drive their trucks on, to educate the people they eventually hire to run the business that makes them all that money, to clean up the environment after they pollute it, or to help 2.5 million people recover from opioid addiction (the result of the horrendous actions of mostly just one corporation).

When corporations don't pay taxes, either someone else does, or the things we need done don't get done. Grover Norquist's tax-free Somalian paradise has roads riddled with potholes, people thirsty for an education they will never get, and an environment that grows worse each day. But at least they don't have those pesky taxes, right?

A recent study found that of the 379 Fortune 500 companies that were profitable in 2018, a whopping 91 paid a federal income tax rate of 0%. That means in the first year after the passage of the Tax Cuts and Jobs Act, nearly a full quarter of profitable Fortune 500 companies ended up paying no federal income taxes whatsoever.[4]

These corporations didn't pull a fast one on the lawmakers who wrote the corporate tax code, and they're not taking advantage of loopholes no one could have predicted. This was the intent of the new Republican tax code, which itself was just the result of a decades-long, corporate, anti-tax campaign that changed the way leaders of both parties approached the corporate tax code. Suffice it to say, in recent memory, the corporate tax code has been much more the result of lobbyists and campaign contributions than of any attempt to craft an effective tax system that asks corporations to pay their fair share.

Ask yourself, How do they get away with it? How do these enormously successful companies pay nothing and leave everyone else holding the bag? Let's dive in.

## Corporate Taxes: The Basics

First, let's clarify that corporations don't pay taxes on all the money they take in every year; they pay taxes only on their profits. If you buy a couch for $1,000, the company you bought it from isn't going to pay taxes on that entire $1,000. They take out all the expenses of their company—including the cost of the raw materials, the cost of transporting the couches, the cost of the ad that convinced you to buy a couch from them instead of their competitor, the cost of the salesperson you bought the couch from or the person who designed and maintains the website you ordered it from, the CEO's salary and company car, and every other little expense and cost along the way.

Because companies pay taxes only on their profits, it is only profitable companies that pay any taxes at all. If a company consistently operates at a loss, there will be no profits to tax. The only companies that have to worry about corporate profits are the ones that are making money and doing well.

A small company, owned by an individual or a family, could make a good product, sell it for a fair price, and pay all the people who work for the company a good wage, and never pay taxes at all because each year they break even. But here we are talking about big corporations, and the name of the game for them is reducing the amount of income that has to be called "profit" when they report their income to the IRS.

From 1993 to 2017, the tax rate on corporate profits was 35%. Most companies paid nowhere near that amount, thanks to a variety of loopholes, but that was what they were technically supposed to pay. Despite never actually paying 35%, corporate executives spent most of those years (and most of the previous decades) complaining about how high the corporate rate was and how it made them unable to compete with corporations from other countries (even though most of the largest and most profitable companies in the world are American). In 2017, their cries were answered, when President Trump and his Republican allies in Congress passed the Tax Cuts and Jobs Act, cutting the corporate rate from 35% down to just 21% while keeping pretty much all the major loopholes that corporations use to avoid paying billions of dollars in taxes. Let's look at some of those tricks.

For much of American history, corporations were considered to have a wide variety of responsibilities—to their workers, to their customers, to the communities they operated in, and to the country as a whole. They may not always have lived up to those responsibilities, but it was generally accepted that corporations had certain social obligations. Cut to 1970, when Milton Friedman, winner of the Nobel Prize for Economics and perhaps one of the most harmful and dangerous economic minds of the modern era, wrote an article claiming that corporations had only one obligation: to make their shareholders as much money as possible, no matter the cost.[2]

In the fifty years since his article's publication, Friedman's stance has become the default position for corporate America. Today it's not just acceptable for a corporation to relentlessly exploit and underpay their workers, use every tax and regulatory loophole their high-priced lawyers can think of, and take advantage of their

customers—it's actually their fiduciary duty to do so. Corporate executives who choose to take care of their workers and their community rather than focus on the short-term earnings that drive up the share price of their company's stock, will likely find themselves out of a job if their company is taken over by a corporate raider or a private-equity firm.

Corporate America desperately needs a culture change, but we can't wait for them to see the light. Some CEOs are starting to recognize and speak out about how destructive the single-minded pursuit of shareholder return is, but if we're going to wait for every corporation to start acting responsibly, we're going to be waiting a long time. Until that point, we need to force them at the very least to give back to the country that guarantees the economic system they operate in.

The following companies are just a few that paid $0 in federal income taxes in 2018:[3]

## Corporate Trick #1: Multinational Money Games: International Profit Shifting

*Multinational corporation* is just a ten-dollar term for a company that conducts business in more than one country. You might expect that if a company does business in more than one country, that company would pay taxes in more than one country. That would be a reasonable expectation, but the devil is in the details. Our system allows corporations to pick and choose where they want to claim income and where they want to claim losses, all of which ends up dramatically shrinking their total tax bill.

Say there's a company that buys coffee beans, hires workers, and rents space in the United States to make coffee and sell it to people in the United States. It also buys coffee beans, hires workers, and rents space in Ireland to make coffee and sell it to people in Ireland. In that scenario, it's more or less straightforward to calculate the profit in the United States and the profit in Ireland, and the company can then pay a percentage of its U.S. profit to the IRS and a percentage of its Irish profits to the Irish version of the IRS.

A large company that serves people coffee might have thirteen or fourteen thousand stores in the United States and five or six dozen stores in Ireland, so one might expect the company to pay a lot of taxes in the United States (at around the 21% corporate rate), and a little bit of taxes in Ireland on the profits from the sixty or so stores in Ireland (at Ireland's 12.5% corporate rate). But that's not how it works at all.

A lot of large companies have what is called intellectual

property—the right to use some piece of knowledge or information—protected by a copyright, a patent, or a trademark. Unlike real property—land, buildings, and other things that are either incredibly difficult to move or cannot be moved at all—intellectual property can be moved easily. For example, the right to publish something can be moved easily. If someone in Australia wanted to publish a book, the right could be granted to them as fast as clicking "send" on an email.

Corporations use this easy transferability of intellectual property to transfer profits away from high-tax countries to low-tax countries without actually changing where they do business at all. For example, a lawyer in Seattle could easily transfer some of Starbucks's intellectual property—such as the company's logo—to Starbucks of Ireland. It's slightly more complicated than that, but let's simplify it for this hypothetical example. Starbucks of Ireland would then technically own that logo, and Starbucks of the United States would have to send royalty payments to Starbucks of Ireland for the privilege of using it. Starbucks doesn't actually send any money or gold or coffee beans or anything else to Ireland. Instead, some nimble-fingered corporate officer in Seattle simply moves billions of dollars of investments from the "Starbucks of USA" account to the "Starbucks of Ireland" account with a quick click of the mouse every year.

Starbucks can make the royalty payments for the use of the logo however much they want and can pay those payments whenever they want. If they make the royalty payments for the use of the logo large enough, they can show none of their profits in the United States and all of their profits in

Ireland, even though they sold far more coffee in the United States. All the profit—and therefore the amount that can be taxed—technically belongs to the company that owns the intellectual property (the logo). Starbucks could end up paying zero income taxes in the United States and all their income taxes in Ireland, dropping the taxes on the money they earn selling coffee in the United States from the U.S. rate of 21% to the Irish rate of 12.5%.

This sets small, noninternational businesses at a huge competitive disadvantage. A big company can afford to have a few properties and smart lawyers in different countries all around the world, picking and choosing where to pay taxes. Mom and Pop's Ice Cream Shop can't afford to hire someone to set up an Irish affiliate to sell a couple of ice cream cones to Irish people, own the rights to their secret butterscotch ice cream recipe, and reap the benefits of a different country's tax system.

## Corporate Trick #2: Giving Away the Store: Our New Territorial Tax System

Before Republicans rewrote the federal tax code, corporations paid a percentage of their total profits in U.S. taxes regardless of where they earned those profits. They received a credit for taxes paid to foreign countries. That's basically the same way it works for people. With the rewrite of the federal tax code, Republicans changed the process for corporations.

Now, post–tax code rewrite, corporations actually pay a lower tax rate on income earned overseas. Instead of paying the standard 21% corporate tax rate, international profits are now taxed by the U.S. government at a 10.5% rate. This "50% off" coupon gives companies a tremendous incentive to shift as much of their profits as possible overseas, rather than keep them in the United States.

Not every piece of the old system has been scrapped, however. Companies still receive credit for 80% of taxes paid to foreign governments, even though the rate they're expected to pay on foreign profits is less than one-third of what they used to owe under the old tax code. (Remember, the old corporate rate used to be 35%.) Because the U.S. corporate rate used to be higher, this credit used to take off only a fraction of a company's U.S. tax obligation. If a company is paying 20% in taxes on the profits they earned in Brazil, for example, they would still owe another 15% to the U.S. government to get to the full 35% they owe. But the U.S. international corporate tax rate is now so low that this credit is often larger than what many corporations owed the United States in the first place. If a corporation earns its profits in a country where the corporate tax rate is even a few percentage points above the now-discounted rate of 10.5% (almost every country in the world), it then ends up paying nothing in U.S. taxes.

The new system is what economists call a "modified territorial tax system," and while it works out great for multinational corporations looking to avoid paying U.S. taxes, it's a bad deal for our country as a whole. We're giving away the store—well, at least the taxes on the store. The old system certainly had its problems, but giving corporations the means to pay virtually no taxes on foreign profits is clearly worse.

"*My bill isn't terribly controversial. It would provide modest tax breaks for people who don't really need them.*"

I earned some money in Greece for a few weeks in 2013, so I had to pay a few thousand dollars in income taxes to the Greek government that year. For my U.S. federal income taxes, I calculated my taxes as usual, including the money I earned in Greece, and at the end I got a credit for the money I paid to the Greek government. The U.S. government still expected me to pay the standard income tax rate, but I was allowed to count the taxes I paid in Greece, so I ended up paying exactly the same total amount of taxes as I would have paid if I had made the same amount working just in New York. This eliminated any incentive I may have had to work in Greece rather than New York. (Well, I did once take off for the weekend to go to the beach in Mykonos, but I meant no *financial* incentive.)

## Corporate Trick #3: Over There, Over There: Relocating Assets Overseas

Not only does the 2017 Tax Cuts and Jobs Act encourage corporations to move their money, their intellectual property, and their corporate headquarters overseas; it actually incentivizes them to move plants and manufacturing facilities to other countries as well, shifting jobs out of the United States.

Under the new law, corporations, which already get a 50%-off coupon on all taxes paid on overseas profits, also get a special accommodation—no taxes below a certain threshold—if they have "tangible assets" (such as factories and equipment) overseas. The United States now taxes only those profits above what is considered a "routine" rate of return on physical assets overseas. For now, that rate of return is set at 10%, meaning that for every $10 million in tangible assets a company owns overseas, the first $1 million it earns in profits is tax free.

The more equipment and factories a company has in other countries, the more tax-free profit it can earn. The law therefore gives corporations a powerful incentive to invest in factories and facilities outside of the United States. Many multinationals plan their investment strategies around increasing their tangible assets in foreign countries specifically to increase the profit they can earn without owing taxes.

Moving a production facility worth hundreds of millions of dollars out of the United States can end up saving a company millions of dollars in taxes each year. For multinationals focused on increasing after-tax profits above all other considerations (i.e., most multinationals), this deal is often too good to pass up. But with these hundreds of millions of dollars of equipment, go many thousands of jobs and the livelihoods of thousands of American workers. Incentivizing multinational corporations to locate their facilities "over there" may be good for shareholders, but it's not good for Americans who need jobs, and it is not good for our tax system.

In June 2018, General Electric (GE) announced that it would be closing its plant in Salem, Virginia, which had been in operation for more than seventy years. The company laid off over 250 workers in Salem during the plant's last few months (at one point the plant employed over 3,000), transferring their positions to GE facilities in India,[5] including a recently built $200 million factory in Pune.[6] Thanks to the Republican tax bill's discounts for tangible assets, building that $200 million factory in India instead of the United States allows GE to avoid paying taxes on $20 million a year in profits.

## Corporate Trick #4: Stocking Up on Loopholes: Stock Options for Executives

Corporations are able to deduct large amounts of money, often in the billions of dollars, from their taxable income by awarding employees with lavish packages of company stock called *options* (because they give the employee the option to purchase the stock at a later date for a predetermined price, which is typically the price at the time that the company makes the award).

Say a company rewards an employee with one thousand options at a $50-a-share price, which the employee can exercise in three years. Three years pass, and the employee decides to exercise those options and buy the shares. At this point, the stock price is $80. The employee buys the stocks at the predetermined $50 price and then immediately sells them for $80 each (the current price). The company gets to deduct the difference between what the employee paid for the stocks ($50 each) and the current value of those stocks ($80 each), even though the company didn't spend that money. This is a simple way for companies to give executives and high-ranking employees massive payouts and significantly reduce their tax burden at the same time, all without spending a dime.

Let's look at this in practice. In 2012, Mark Zuckerberg exercised options he had gotten in the early days of Facebook. He bought sixty million shares of Facebook at his option price of 6¢ each at a time when the stock was trading at $38 per share.[7] When Zuckerberg bought those shares, the company got to deduct the multibillion-dollar difference between the value of what Zuckerberg bought (sixty million shares times $38) and

*"Listen—we just stay silent and look remote and concerned and dignified, and we keep the damn bonuses."*

*"To representation without taxation!"*

what he paid (sixty million shares times 6¢). Zuckerberg exercising his stock options canceled out Facebook's $1.1 billion in reported profits for 2012 and actually qualified the company for $429 million in refunds from the federal government.[8]

These kinds of payouts are essentially free to companies. Giving away extra shares of stock costs a company nothing. This kind of tax break incentivizes companies to give their executives massive stock-based compensation packages, driving up executive pay to sometimes absurd levels. Paying a salary or cash payout, on the other hand, requires actual money.

## Corporate Trick #5: Look Fast! Oh, You Missed It: Accelerated Depreciation

The corporate tax code is very complicated. That's partially by design. If you make it difficult for the average person to understand how corporate taxes even work, it's easier to sneak tax breaks into the tax code without the general public getting upset. And as long as corporations have the resources to hire squadrons of tax lawyers and accountants, they're fine with complexity hiding the giveaways they're getting.

One such giveaway is a tax break known as accelerated depreciation. It's the single largest domestic tax break available to American corporations.

Remember, businesses are taxed only on their profits, and to determine their profits, companies subtract their expenses from their revenues. If you earn $100 and have $50 of costs, you're taxed on only the $50 of profit. Sometimes costs and expenses are easily quantifiable. Say a company sells a novelty fake mustache for $10, and it costs the business exactly $5 for the raw materials and labor. That $5 would be deducted from the company's $10 in taxable income. That's easy to calculate.

But what do companies do when they have costs that are harder to quantify on an annual basis, for example if that company buys a truck to bring its mustaches from its factory to department stores? That truck is a long-term investment that costs significant money up front but will add value for the company over time. Depreciation allows companies to deduct the cost of these kinds of long-term investments over a period of time, to allow for the fact that assets depreciate in value over time. Say a company pays $100,000 for a new truck. On the balance sheet, the company is no different before and after the purchase of that truck. The company used to have $100,000 in cash, and now it has a $100,000 truck. It just replaced $100,000 of cash with a different asset that is worth the same. As the truck is used, however, it becomes less valuable, and that loss in value counts as an expense when it comes to calculating taxes.

As the lifetime of the investment passes, the company uses up the value of the truck. For every year that it operates, it loses one more year of future operation, and loses a commensurate portion of the original value. That loss in value is called depreciation. As depreciation occurs, companies can deduct the corresponding fraction of lost value from their taxable income every year. If the truck costs $100,000 and is expected to last for five years, the company can claim $20,000 as an expense each year and deduct that amount from its taxable income.

Under the new federal tax code, companies are allowed to deduct the total value of their depreciating assets *on an accelerated basis*. This allows companies to count the full cost of many assets as an expense much earlier than it actually takes for those assets to lose all their value. The tax regulations contain a comprehensive set of rules on how much depreciation companies can deduct on their tax returns. In almost all cases, the allowed depreciation is much quicker than the rate at which those assets actually wear out. A company might be able to deduct the entire cost of a $100,000 truck over five years because the government says that the truck's value is entirely used up in five years, even if the truck actually lasts for ten years. There's a significant gap between "real" depreciation, or how quickly an asset actually wears out, versus the tax code's depreciation rates. That gap represents a major boon to companies making capital investments.

## A Dollar Today Is Worth More Than a Dollar Tomorrow

While corporations would eventually be able to deduct the full value of their assets no matter what, allowing them to make those deductions earlier ends up saving those companies a significant amount of money. Pushing back tax payments is valuable, thanks to the time value of money, which simply means that a dollar today is worth more than a dollar tomorrow.

Taking deductions earlier rather than later allows companies to redirect money that would have gone to tax payments into other profitable investments, earning them more money in the long run. Assume conservatively that a company can earn a 5% return on its investments, a dollar today can lead to much more than a dollar down the line. Let's look at the math.

Companies that take advantage of accelerated depreciation are able to defer tax payments for years, essentially receiving a free, no-interest loan from the federal government. Scaled up from this example in the thousands of dollars to the billions of dollars (the actual amount at stake), this ends up being a massive amount of money. The Joint Committee on Taxation, Congress's bipartisan taxation estimator, calculated that between 2017 and 2021, accelerated depreciation would cost the U.S. government $331 billion.[10]

## Accelerated Depreciation at Work

In anticipation of the end of the Postal Service as we know it, Zippee, an overnight delivery company, buys ten trucks, spending a total of half a million dollars. When tax time rolls around, Zippee's accountants use accelerated depreciation to "expense" the trucks, deducting the entire cost of the trucks as depreciation in the first year they're in use. By deducting the full $500,000 cost of the trucks from their taxable profits that year, Zippee saves $105,000 in taxes (21% of $500,000). With an extra $105,000 in after-tax profits to work with, Zippee's CFO puts that money into another investment that earns 5% each year. Here's how that investment's value grows:

Year 1: $105,000
Year 2: $110,250
Year 3: $115,763
Year 4: $121,551
Year 5: $127,628
Year 6: $134,010
Year 7: $140,710
Year 8: $147,746
Year 9: $155,133
Year 10: $162,889

Now compare that to Sloze Shipping and Handling, which buys the same trucks for the same price, but at a less zippy depreciation schedule: they deduct the cost of the trucks over ten years. Ultimately, they get the same overall tax benefit, but at $10,500 a year instead of all at once. With that $10,500 a year, Sloze's CFO makes the same invest-ment as Zippee with a 5% return, but at a slower rate over time instead of all at once up front.

Year 1: $10,500

Year 2: $21,525

Year 3: $33,101

Year 4: $45,256

Year 5: $58,019

Year 6: $71,420

Year 7: $85,491

Year 8: $100,266

Year 9: $115,779

Year 10: $132,068

Thanks to accelerated depreciation, Zippee is able to earn almost 25% more over ten years than Sloze Shipping and Handling.

### "Bonus Depreciation": Full Expensing

In 2002, Congress and the Bush administration passed a law that allowed "bonus depreciation," which moved up the time line under which corporations could deduct certain assets. The law allowed some categories of assets to have up to 50% of their entire value deducted in the year they were purchased.[9] This was intended at the time to be a temporary provision, but thanks to a well-funded effort by corporate lobbyists, Congress kept extending it.

As if being able to immediately deduct 50% of an investment's value weren't enough, in 2017 congressional Republicans and President Trump made expanding accelerated depreciation a priority in their rewrite of the tax code. Corporations are now able to deduct 100% of the cost of many types of assets *in the first year that they're put into service.* (This immediate deduction is known as "expensing.")

When it was passed into law in 2017, this provision was set to expire after five years, but, much like the Bush administration's bonus-depreciation change, this provision is in the sights of corporate lobbyists, who are hard at work pressuring members of Congress on both sides of the aisle to renew it before it expires in 2022.

## Focus on the Big Picture, Not the Details

Each of these loopholes in the personal and corporate tax code is a problem individually, but the way they all work together is the real issue that needs fixing. The capital gains tax rate, the carried-interest loophole, the stepped-up basis, stock options, the pass-through deduction, accelerated depreciation, and dozens of other loopholes and problems with our tax code all end up making richer people even richer and creating the destabilizing levels of inequality from which our country is currently suffering.

These various loopholes and schemes work together to make the rich richer and leave everyone else behind. Correcting our system will take a similarly systemic approach. But we can't fix things until we acknowledge what's broken, beginning with exposing the lies that serve as the intellectual justification for the whole ridiculous set up.

## How Amazon Ends Up Paying $0 in Federal Taxes
### (by Morris)

In 2018, Amazon earned $11.26 billion in profits. That same year, Amazon paid $0 in federal income taxes. How is that possible? Let's look at exactly how Amazon used all the loopholes available to them.

According to the law, the U.S. federal corporate income tax rate is 21%, so one might think that on profits of $11.26 billion, Amazon would pay U.S. federal income taxes of about $2.36 billion. Not so.

### International Profit Shifting

According to Amazon, over 99% of their profits were earned in the United States, with just $104 million of that $11.26 billion earned in other countries. However, Amazon paid $563 million of corporate income taxes in other countries—an apparent income tax rate of 541%.

Clearly, Amazon is not paying taxes of more than five times its profit in those countries. Instead, Amazon is paying taxes in foreign countries at very low rates on some of its *U.S. profit*, by claiming that those profits were earned in other countries.

### Stock-Option Deductions

Amazon also avoids taxes by using the old stock-options standby. Amazon's highly paid professional employees (not Mr. Bezos, however) are sometimes granted stock options. That means that, as part of their annual pay for a given year, these employees have the "option" to buy stock later at the price of the stock when the employee first

*Disclaimer: My family and I own around a million dollars' worth of Amazon stock. The source for this analysis is note 9 to Amazon's financial statements for the year 2018 which is on pages 62 and 63 of Amazon's Form 10-K filed with the SEC on February 1, 2019.[11]*

got the option. In 2015 an engineer might be given the option to buy one thousand shares of Amazon stock at the 2015 price of $500 per share, three years later. Because the stock was trading at $2,000 per share by 2018, that employee would gain the change in price on one thousand shares, making $1,500 multiplied by one thousand shares, or $1.5 million dollars.

This full amount would count as an expense to Amazon, which could take a tax deduction of $1.5 million—even though Amazon *never actually spent any money.* (In fact, the company received $500,000 from the sale of the stock to the employee.)

### Accelerated Depreciation

Amazon arranges its affairs and its investments so that it gets tax deductions every year related to future expenses, paying taxes only eventually. In some cases "eventually" can stretch into forever. And the amount deferred can keep growing.

Imagine that you charge stuff on your credit card. If the bank keeps increasing your credit limit every year, you can essentially buy stuff and never pay for it. One of the main ways Amazon does that is by accelerated depreciation. When Amazon buys something to use in its business (server computers for its data centers, say), part of the price of those computers is assigned to each year that the computers will be in use. If the computers will be used for four years, Amazon can assign one-fourth of the price of the computer to each year.

Under accelerated-depreciation rules, however, for *tax* purposes, Amazon can assign most of the price to the first year. So in that first year, Amazon might be making a profit, but because of that tax deduction, the depreciated value of the computers lowers Amazon's profits on its tax returns, eradicating some or all of Amazon's tax bill.

# On Lies and Liars (By Morris)

*Once you give up your integrity, the rest is a piece of cake.*

—J.R. Ewing

I really try to think the best about people, or to remain neutral if I can't do that. When politicians make decisions that are very good for their contributors and very bad for regular people, I like to believe that it is because the politician is confused or has been misled.

I remember being at a cocktail party once with a U.S. senator, who remarked that it was good that he was not a self-funder (meaning wealthy enough to fund his own campaign without needing donations) because it was only at fundraising events that he got to see "regular people." I looked around a New York City apartment filled with millionaires and wondered what in the world he was talking about. If this is his definition of regular people, I thought, we have big problems. News flash America: we have big problems.

One of our biggest problems is that our campaign system ensures that most politicians spend an enormous amount of time hearing the perspectives of very wealthy people and very little time hearing the perspectives of everybody else. Wealthy people tend to talk with politicians about ways to make the economy work very well for wealthy people. I assume regular people would, likewise, talk with politicians about what would make the economy work well for them. Unfortunately, you don't find that many regular people in multimillion-dollar Park Avenue apartments.

They say the worst lies are the ones that people tell themselves. That is certainly true for rich people in the tax debate. A lot of wealthy people have been so wealthy for so long that they have lost all perspective. That's the problem with being rich and successful. If you're doing well, it's human nature to assume that you've earned it—that you've "made the right choices in life."

Paul Piff, a famous social psychologist, once conducted a behavioral experiment where he observed the interpersonal dynamics taking place over several rigged Monopoly games. In each of the rigged games, one player was given a significant advantage over the others, such as starting with twice as much money or getting to roll three dice instead of two. Just fifteen minutes into the rigged game, the privileged players began to behave more aggressively toward their fellow players. They spoke louder, moved their pieces more forcefully, and demonstrated other "displays of power." After the game, one advantaged player was overheard explaining to a group of disadvantaged players his strategy for winning, as though his victory were actually the result of his quick thinking rather than the fact that he got twice as much money as the others every time he passed "Go."[2] A lot of rich people are like that guy.

Next time you hear a wealthy person opining about the economy, please keep in mind, just because the wealthy person believes fervently in what they're saying, that doesn't mean they're right. Wealthy people seem to have a special knack for being entirely convinced of their own perspective. Let's hope this chapter provides some gentle clarification for our hopefully–well–intentioned–but–quite–misguided, wealthy friends.

You've probably seen that picture of an iceberg that shows both the small part above the water and the enormous part hidden beneath the waterline. The next time you read a news article about how tax cuts for the rich are good for the economy and therefore good for you, I hope you will think of that iceberg. As a regular citizen, you see one small part of the anti-tax campaign in the media, but you may never witness the incredible size of the marketing and lobbying apparatus, funded by millionaires and billionaires, that's going on below the surface to help the richest people on the planet become even wealthier by avoiding taxes.

The reason rich people have to spend so much money promoting their point of view is because much of what passes for a coherent argument in the anti-tax debate is illogical on its face. Let's look at a few of the biggest lies rich people tell themselves.

## Lie #1: Corporate tax cuts create jobs.

Randall Stephenson, CEO of AT&T, was one of the biggest public cheerleaders for corporate tax cuts leading up to the passage of the new Republican tax code. Stephenson promised that cutting corporate tax rates would lead to huge job growth because the correlation between tax cuts and job creation was "very, very tight."[3]

When he made this assertion, Stephenson must have been referring to companies other than AT&T. From 2008 to 2015, using a variety of loopholes and tax breaks, AT&T paid an effective corporate tax rate of 8%, well below the standard corporate rate of 35%.[4] With such a low tax rate, AT&T must have created tons of jobs then, right? Wrong. The company actually cut nearly eighty thousand jobs during that time[5] and then used some of the money from the layoffs and its low tax rate to buy back $34 billion worth of AT&T stock,[6] a move that helped inflate Stephenson's personal net worth quite a bit. Stephenson made over $80 million in five years as the head of AT&T,[7] receiving $32 million from the company in 2019 alone.[8]

Stephenson may have been a convincing spokesperson for the anti-taxers, but he was wrong about everything he said. Was he lying? Or just confused? Maybe Randall Stephenson had forgotten that he had cut eighty thousand jobs when his company's tax rate was in the single digits. Maybe he really believed that if only his company's taxes were lower, he would hire people instead of firing eighty thousand of them.

We cannot see inside Randall Stephenson's head; however,

we can see inside a recent report from the Institute for Policy Studies that studied the correlation between tax cuts and job growth at some of the country's biggest companies. The authors of the study looked at the job-creation records of the ninety-two publicly held U.S. corporations that reported a U.S. profit every year from 2008 to 2015, and that also paid less than 20% in federal income tax. (Remember, during those years the corporate rate was 35%.)[9] Those ninety-two profitable companies paid much less in taxes than they were expected to, so according to the people promoting corporate tax cuts as a job-creation strategy, those companies must have employed more people than did other companies that paid more in taxes, right?

Wrong. Across the economy, the average private-sector company increased the number of people they employed by 6% during that time period. The ninety-two profitable, tax-dodging companies, on the other hand, had their employment levels *drop* by an average of 1%. The companies that paid less in taxes actually *shed jobs overall* as the economy grew. Despite their low tax rate, more than half of the companies studied—48 out of 92—cut jobs, downsizing by a total of 483,000 jobs. The next time someone tells you the correlation between tax cuts and job creation is "very tight," tell them about Randall Stephenson.

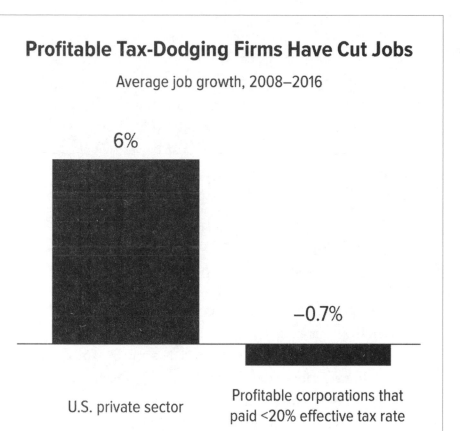

**Profitable Tax-Dodging Firms Have Cut Jobs**

Average job growth, 2008–2016

6%

−0.7%

U.S. private sector

Profitable corporations that
paid <20% effective tax rate

SOURCE: BLS, INSTITUTE ON TAXATION AND ECONOMIC POLICY, 10-K REPORTS

**A** few years ago, there was a long feature article in the *New York Times* about the dreadful conditions in a homeless shelter in New York City.[1] I was at a cocktail party in a huge apartment overlooking Central Park the night it came out, and I asked our host what he thought about the article, which focused on the story of an eleven-year-old child, stuck in the shelter system. My host responded that people needed to take more responsibility for the choices they made in life. Keep in mind that we were sipping our drinks in a multimillion-dollar apartment in a building he owned because his family bought it before he was born. I wonder how much responsibility my multimillionaire host had for the choices he made when he was eleven.

## Lie #2: Private-equity investors are job creators (and deserve a special tax break).

The private-equity industry, which specializes in taking over businesses, reorganizing them, extracting value, and then selling them off, says it deserves special tax breaks, such as the carried-interest loophole, because the industry is a job creator. The industry is not a job creator.

Let's consider what happened when KKR and Bain Capital, two private-equity firms, took over Toys "R" Us in 2005. Lobbyists for the private-equity industry claimed in 2010 that this was a success story, that they had saved the company, pointing to the 62,000 people Toys "R" Us employed under their management as an example of private equity's job creation bona fides.[10] Well, it's a telling example, but probably not in the way they meant it.

Prior to the private-equity takeover, Toys "R" Us was in healthy financial shape, with annual profits of $252 million, cash on hand of $2.1 billion, and outstanding long-term debt of $1.9 billion.[11] More importantly, with respect to job creation, before the private-equity barons got their hands on the company, Toys "R" Us employed *97,000* people at its peak in 2004.[12]

In 2005, KKR and Bain (along with real-estate firm Vornado) paid $6.6 billion for Toys "R" Us. The private-equity investors then closed stores around the country, so they could sell the buildings the stores were located in, and laid off thousands of people.[13]

A significant amount of that $6.6 billion used to buy the company was raised through debt, debt that was then added to the Toys "R" Us books, debt that kept the company from properly investing in online retail at a time when big-box stores were facing more challenges, debt that forced the once-profitable company into bankruptcy in 2017.[14] By the time the "job creating" private-equity folks were done with the company, they had shut down all of its 735 U.S. stores and loaded its once-positive balance sheet with $7.9 billion in debt.[15]

This left tens of thousands of workers without jobs and without the severance they were promised.[16] (Toy "R" Us employees eventually recovered a few million dollars in severance through the court system, but those settlements fell far short of the $75 million they were owed.) The investors meanwhile scooped up as much as $470 million overall since the 2005 purchase.[17] In this instance (and many others), private-equity "job creators" destroyed a viable company and cost nearly one hundred thousand people their jobs. If this is what the private equity business does, how can it argue it deserves a tax break? Give me a break.

## Lie #3: People who invest in the stock market are job creators (and deserve a special tax break).

Most members of the 1% make the majority of their money through investments rather than through ordinary income from a job. They use their wealth to buy stocks or bonds or some other financial asset and wait for those assets to increase in value. Like their friends in private equity, stock-market investors also like to believe they are "job creators." They are not.

I'm an investor who lives off millions of dollars' worth of investments. I haven't actually worked in years; I let my money make me money. Do you know how many jobs I have created with my investments? Exactly zero. (Maybe one, if you count the person helping us write this book.)

Jobs are created by consumer demand for products and services, not investment dollars. Thousands of people are employed making iPhones for the more than 175 million people who bought an iPhone last year (earning far too little, but that's a topic for another book). I'm an investor in Apple to the tune of hundreds of thousands of dollars in stock. But while I benefit from Apple doing well, I certainly don't deserve the credit for creating the jobs of those people employed making iPhones. They have their jobs because of the millions of people who want to buy the product they're making.

In fact, Apple itself doesn't even benefit from me buying Apple stock. I, like almost everyone else who owns Apple stock, bought it from another investor, not directly from the company—I've never paid Apple a dime (aside from buying an iPhone and a few other things). I've only ever benefited from Apple's growth; I've done nothing to actually contribute to it. If an Apple employee wants to thank someone for their job, they should thank the next person they see talking on an iPhone, not the next person they see who owns Apple stock.

## Lie #4: Business owners are job creators.

Rich people claim they use their wealth to build businesses and create jobs, and that if you tax them more, you'll be taking away money they would otherwise be using to create jobs. They argue that taxing business owners kills jobs and hurts the economy. It does not.

Yes, businesspeople start companies and hire employees, but those jobs do not exist as a result of the benevolence or genius of the company's founder—they exist because of consumer demand. Customers buy products or services provided by a company, and the money they spend allows that company to hire employees to produce and sell those products or services. The founder of the company plays an important role in initiating and organizing this process, but ultimately the employment of everyone within that company is dependent on the continued demand for what it sells. If consumers stop buying the company's product, the company collapses, and everyone loses their jobs. Luckily, the customers—the real job creators—still exist, even if the company making that product doesn't. Don't worry, this is okay, at least in the long run. Before too long another entrepreneur will come along and organize a company to fulfill the consumer demand (and make some money in the process).

The people creating jobs at a grocery store aren't the executives of the store, they're the customers buying groceries every week. The rich people at the top organize the process of creating goods and selling them to customers, but they are more like surfers riding a wave than water creators. The only thing that actually creates and sustains jobs is consumer demand, which requires a strong and prosperous middle class, not massive tax cuts for the rich. As Ben Cohen, the founder of Ben & Jerry's, says, "There's only so much Chunky Monkey one rich guy can eat."[18]

Yes, some entrepreneurs have developed a product or service so revolutionary that it created an entire industry out of nothing that wouldn't otherwise have existed. But most other rich people got rich by taking advantage of existing market forces. They may have refined some process or created a slightly better mousetrap, but growing your own business by taking a chunk of market share away from a competitor doesn't mean that you're creating jobs. Those jobs, or similar ones in another company, would have existed regardless; they just happen to be at your company now instead of someone else's. Apple may have kickstarted the smartphone boom with its first iPhone, but in a world without Apple, some other company would have gotten there eventually. That market, and those jobs, would still exist, even if it was Pear or Kumquat or some other company that had dominated the smartphone space.

# ECONOMICS 101:

## We can't have a consumer-based economy if consumers can't afford to consume.

Some companies actually destroy jobs

Many of the most celebrated "job creators" in our economy are actually responsible for the destruction of more jobs than they've created. Business owners and investors get rich through enacting efficiencies, and part of making a company more efficient is cutting out overhead, which often means either cutting wages or cutting jobs. The fewer people you can employ to get a job done, the more money you're going to be left with.

Take Jeff Bezos and Amazon, for example. Amazon employs about eight hundred thousand people, so some confused people may consider Bezos an incredible job creator. He isn't. Amazon's jobs didn't appear out of thin air when Bezos waved his wand and called on the gods of job creation. Amazon's growth actually has led to the closure of thousands of small bookstores, mom and pop stores, and other local businesses. A clean bottom is not a new idea, and neither is buying toilet paper; before Amazon, other companies sold toilet paper too. Much of Amazon's growth has come at the expense of normal brick-and-mortar retailers and other online-retail companies. And because much of Amazon's edge has been its incredible efficiency, the number of jobs it has created as it absorbs market share from other companies is outweighed by the number that it's destroyed.[19]

## Lie #5: Taxing capital gains discourages investment.

As we discussed earlier, rich people claim that if we raise taxes on investors by increasing the capital gains tax rate, people will stop investing. According to them, rich investors *need* a special tax rate, or it just won't be worth their money to invest, and without their money, the economy will grind to a halt.

Now this is just plain silly. There actually is math on this exam. The people claiming that investors won't invest if you raise their taxes do not know what they are talking about. Wealthy investors are going to invest no matter what the capital gains tax rate is. They don't need an extra tax incentive to invest because they don't really have any other options.

The choice rich people face every day is whether to stay out of the market and end the year with the same amount of money they started the year with, or invest their money so that even after they've paid taxes, they end the year with more money than they started with. This is a no-brainer. The tax rate has no effect whatsoever on the decision to invest; it affects only how much additional money you will make from investing. The only way to grow your wealth is to invest, regardless of the tax rate.

Capital gains taxes come out of the profit you earn on your investments. No matter how high the tax rate is, it's only ever going to come out of your *profits*. If your investments have done well enough for you to pay capital gains taxes, you will come out ahead of someone who just kept their money in cash, no matter what the tax rate is. Even with a 90% tax rate, if you earn an extra $1 million a year in capital gains, you're going to end up $100,000 ahead of someone who didn't invest at all.

Ask yourself, Would you rather keep 40%, 30%, or even 20% of something, or 100% of nothing? You do the math.

## Lie #6: Rich people's charity does so much good in the world that if we tax them, they won't have enough money to help poor people.

Lots of rich people want to see their name on a fancy building. Fewer rich people want to see their name on a sewage-treatment plant. And that, in a nutshell, is why we tax people instead of relying solely on rich people's charity. All that toilet paper that Jeff Bezos is selling has to go somewhere you know. Properly functioning sewage systems are essential to a strong, fragrant society, so we tax people to ensure we have these systems, as it is doubtful that many rich people would choose to fund sewage-treatment plants on their own.

Now, from time to time, a story about a very wealthy individual doing something very kind with their money goes viral. Billionaire Robert F. Smith paid off the student debt of the entire Morehouse College class of 2019. Patagonia CEO Rose Marcario pledged to donate the company's entire $10 million tax cut to nonprofit organizations fighting climate change. Bill Gates pledged over $4 billion to fight malaria around the globe in 2017. These are extraordinary stories.

Unfortunately, these stories create the impression that a few people with big hearts and bigger bank accounts can fix society's problems. But the scale of private charitable giving is tiny compared to our society's needs. Total charitable giving for all Americans combined in 2017 (itemized on tax returns) amounted to $269 billion. That's a lot of money, but it is not even close to the size of the federal budget, which typically hovers around $4 trillion.

It's also not all coming from the rich. We're conditioned to think of rich people as extremely generous because the media loves to cover stories of wealthy people donating really large amounts of money, but as a percentage of their total wealth, the ultrawealthy are actually less generous than normal Americans are. Jeff Bezos donated $690,000 in January 2020 to help Australia recover from a series of devastating brushfires. That seems really generous—at first. But when you consider that, by some calculations, his net worth increases by about $230,000 per minute, that figure seems much less impressive.[20] An accurate headline would read something like "Bezos Gives Three Minutes of His Time to Stop Brush Fires." When you put it that way, does he really deserve to be Outback Hero of the Month?

The twenty richest Americans donated about $8.7 billion to charity in 2018—less than 1% of their total net worth. Take away Bill Gates and Warren Buffett, the most generous of the top twenty, and the other eighteen ended up giving just $2.8 billion, or 0.32% of their total net worth. That's less than the national average—0.33% of household wealth.[21]

"So what?" some people might say. "They still gave $8.7 billion, that's a lot of money." And it is a lot of money. But it's nowhere near enough money to fix large systemic problems. More importantly, it's nowhere near as much money as we could raise by taxing them more. Some estimates put the amount potentially raised by Senator Elizabeth Warren's wealth tax at $200 billion a year.[22] Our society would be much better off with an extra $200 billion a year for the community to decide how to use through a process determined by a representative democracy.

The scope of the challenges facing the American people is vast, and the sporadic generosity of even the most generous rich people is no substitute for systemic solutions to systemic problems. Many of the solutions to the problems plaguing this country are simply out of the reach of private individuals. They require the type of action that only the federal government can provide.

## Charity Isn't Always So Selfless

Even when rich people are spending a lot of money on "charity," they're often not actually doing a lot of good, because charity means a very different thing to rich people than it does to most Americans. Rich people aren't just dropping their millions into a big Salvation Army pot. There is an entire ecosystem of charitable giving that exists not to help the less fortunate, but to extend the influence of the rich and powerful.

Instead of donating to other charities the way normal people do, many of the ultrarich create their own charities, by setting up private foundations or donor-advised funds (DAFs) that they control. By donating to their own foundations instead of to established charities, they still get to deduct their giving from their taxes, but they have much more say over how and when their money is used, or even whether it ever gets used at all.

There's another problem too. While billionaires may give a substantial gift to their foundation or their DAF, and take the tax break on the donated money, that doesn't mean they are actually spending that money on worthy endeavors—or spending it at all. In many cases, that money sits for years, even decades, before being spent, despite the fact that the donor already received the tax break.

Foundations are required to pay out only 5% of their total assets every year, and DAFs have no payout requirements at all. This means rich people can make a big PR splash by establishing and funding a foundation or DAF, take a massive deduction from their taxes, and then not spend the money on anything actually charitable until some unspecified point in the future.

Giving rich people, even when they do spend money, total control over their charitable giving can lead to that money being spent in unsavory ways. It's common in the philanthropic world to see personal foundations that don't really do any actual charity work but are instead used to:

- do favors for the donor's friends or family by giving them high-paying positions managing the foundation,
- improve the donor's reputation by making donations that earn them good PR,
- advocate for public policies that benefit the donor financially or otherwise, or
- spend $60,000 to purchase portraits of the foundation's founder (remember the Trump Foundation?).

"Yes, we're a charity tackling skyrocketing income inequality, but we're also a charity that should be saying 'I love my billionaire funder.'"

## Reputation Laundering

Even when a rich person's charitable giving is being well spent, it's often being used as a cover for other, more toxic behavior that harms people far more than the charity is helping them. It's a classic PR move: make a big splashy donation to something good so people stop paying attention to the bad things you did. Journalist Anand Giridharadas details this kind of "reputation laundering" in his book *Winners Take All: The Elite Charade of Changing the World*, in which he explains how much of modern philanthropy is designed to cover up the sins of the top 1%.

As Giridharadas writes, behind the haze of buzzwords such as "win-win," "giving back," and "social purpose," wealthy "thought leaders" pour millions into gestures of generosity while failing to address the structural issues behind the problems they're "fixing." At best, these would-be saviors suffer from a glaring poverty of understanding; at worst, they knowingly leverage the optics of generosity to make it easier to hold on to their own privilege.

Whether it's ExxonMobil giving to disaster-relief funds after climate change–fueled hurricanes ravage the Gulf Coast, or Bill Gates donating huge sums to his foundation during the eighteen-month period that Microsoft was the target of a federal antitrust lawsuit, the wealthy use charitable giving as a shield for their bad behavior. Lucky for them, all this reputation laundering comes with a tax deduction.

## Lie #7: It's their money.

Rich people love to talk about how important it is for hard-working people to be able to keep their hard-earned money. That's the American dream, they say, where with grit and determination you can succeed completely on your own.

Let's be clear, no rich person got to where they are today without a lot of help. First of all, a significant number of rich people did literally nothing to earn their wealth aside from being born into the right family. Between 35% and 45% of all the wealth in America is inherited.[23] Even those who didn't inherit billions often had some sort of head start from well-off and successful parents. Mark Zuckerberg—now one of the wealthiest people in the world—did not start life as a billionaire, but he did start with parents who could give him a stipend for years and invest hundreds of thousands of dollars in his company at the beginning.

Mr. Zuckerberg may be brilliant, and he may work really hard, but he also had significant advantages that most Americans do not have. Bill Gates, Jeff Bezos, and many other titans of industry also started if not on third base, then at least well outfitted for the game.

Even those who didn't have a head start owe much of their wealth to the economic system and infrastructure that our government creates and maintains. Zuckerberg's and Bezos's businesses are possible only because of the internet—which was developed and paid for by the government (it used to be called the ARPANET, which stood for the Advanced Research Project Agency Network). Businesses in America are able to move their goods thanks to roads funded by the government, and hire people to work for them thanks to a workforce largely educated in government-funded public schools. No one becomes successful in a vacuum.

## Lie #8: Politicians care just as much about their constituents as they do about their donors.

If you want to have the opportunity to serve the people, you'd better learn how to suck up to the millionaires and billionaires you need to fund your campaign. Most members of Congress spend hours each day on the phone calling donors and asking them for money. Many actually spend more time fundraising than they do legislating.[24] It's pretty easy to predict what happens when nearly every member of Congress spends a significant number of their waking hours calling, meeting, talking with, and thinking about rich people—they start passing laws that favor rich people over everyone else.

Some experts estimate that political ad spending reached about $10 billion in the 2020 election.[25] And while some, such as Representative Alexandria Ocasio-Cortez and Senator Bernie Sanders, have had success soliciting small-dollar donations, the quickest, simplest, and easiest path to raising a lot of money is to ask rich people for it. The top 0.01% alone—the top 1% of the 1%—account for over one-third of all political spending.[26] In 2018, just the top one hundred donors accounted for over $662 million in Super PAC contributions.[27]

Even if a lawmaker has the best of intentions, her idea of what's best for the country and her district is almost certainly

# Model Daily Schedule - DC

☑ 4 hours — Call Time

☑ 1-2 hours — Constituent Visits

☑ 2 hours — Committee/Floor

☑ 1 hour — Strategic Outreach
Breakfasts, Meet & Greets, Press

☑ 1 hour — Recharge Time

SOURCE: DCCC Powerpoint to Freshman Lawmakers, 2017

going to be skewed by the people she interacts with daily. I personally get at least one or two calls a day from members of Congress, and I talk with at least a few every month at some fundraiser or event. I guarantee that if I wanted to talk with your congressperson, I would have an easier time scheduling a call than you would, even though I'm not a constituent.

When politicians talk more with people like me and less with their constituents, they naturally start to have a skewed perspective. If they hear two dozen business owners say some new regulation is going to kill jobs and hurt the economy and just one low-income worker say that same regulation would help protect them on the job, then of course those two dozen voices are going to outweigh the one worker's perspective, even if there are actually many more low-wage workers than business owners in the politician's district.

## Straight-Up Corruption

Sometimes politicians do things to help rich people because their perspective is so skewed from talking with rich people all day that they think what's good for the rich really is good for the country as a whole. But sometimes the politicians are just blatantly corrupt. They aren't stupid. Politicians know that if they sponsor a bill a donor likes or vote a certain way, they can expect to see more money roll in. It doesn't have to be explicitly stated for both sides to know exactly what's going on.

A donor may ask a politician to do them a favor by slipping a small change into a piece of legislation, and in return that donor gives generously to the politician's reelection campaign. Sometimes it's more subtle, a light hint that special attention

"BUT IT WOULD BE RUDE TO RAISE TAXES ON MY FRIENDS."

paid to a certain loophole would be greatly appreciated. Sometimes it happens without the donor saying anything at all, as the lawmaker makes proactive decisions to work on legislation that he knows will make his donor base happy.

Everyone taking part in this game is so confident in their ability to keep it going that they don't even try to hide it. As the new Republican tax code was moving through Congress, several Republican lawmakers said the quiet part out loud. Senator Lindsay Graham told a reporter that if the Republican party couldn't pass the tax cuts bill, "the financial contributions will stop." Former Representative Chris Collins (who eventually pled guilty to insider trading and lying to the FBI)[28] said, "My donors are basically saying, 'Get it done or don't ever call me again.'"[29]

## For the Rich, It's an Investment

Paul Ryan's joint fundraising committee got a $500,000 check for his PAC from one of the Koch brothers, Charles Koch, and his wife just days after the new Republican tax code passed the House, which could be interpreted as a job-well-done bonus.[31] The two brothers pledged $20 million to help market the tax bill to American voters. A group affiliated with the Kochs launched a national "job creators" bus tour, doubling down on one of the most transparently absurd claims of the anti-taxers' marketing campaign. That's a lot of money, but it was a profitable investment. By one estimate, Koch Industries could have earned around $1.4 *billion* off the changes to the tax code.[32]

This is how rich people think about their political spending,

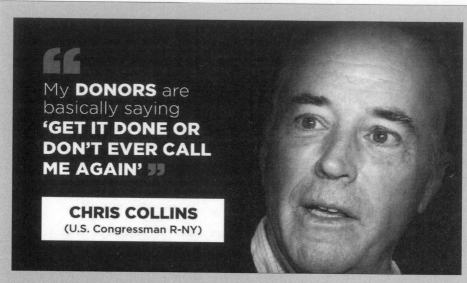

"My **DONORS** are basically saying **'GET IT DONE OR DON'T EVER CALL ME AGAIN'**"

**CHRIS COLLINS**
(U.S. Congressman R-NY)

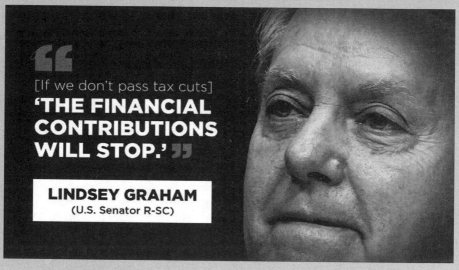

"[If we don't pass tax cuts] **'THE FINANCIAL CONTRIBUTIONS WILL STOP.'**"

**LINDSEY GRAHAM**
(U.S. Senator R-SC)

as an investment in future earnings. So they'll spend millions on direct campaign contributions, PACs, Super PACs, and independent media campaigns on subjects that range from abortion to immigration, all to get lawmakers with a tax-cutting agenda elected. (Getting voters fired up over social issues to support candidates who want to cut taxes for the rich is a classic part of the conservatives' playbook.) As you read this, billionaires across America are paying people at universities, think tanks, media organizations, political campaigns, Super PACs, and advocacy groups to sell you on one idea and one idea alone: *Tax cuts for rich people are good for regular people.* That sentence is so absurd on its face that they're clearly going to need to spend millions to sell you on it. But with *billions* of their money at stake, it's money they're willing to spend.

Coca-Cola spends an average of roughly $4 billion on marketing every year. The company has net operating revenues of around $30 billion a year. If you could spend $4 to make $30 would you do it? If you could spend $4,000 to make $30,000, would you? How about $4 million to make $30 million? See, now you're getting it. Tax cuts for rich people are just like Coca-Cola: bad for you and profitable for them.

## Evidence That the System Is Broken

In addition to anecdotal evidence, research shows that when it comes to passing laws, Congress members pay much more attention to what rich people want than they do to what their constituents want. In fact, data show that the general population's view of a policy has no effect at all on whether or not it ends up becoming law. The only thing that matters is how much support a policy has among the wealthy elite.

A study by Princeton professor Martin Gilens[30] shows that between the 1980s and the 2010s, policies supported by the rich ended up being passed into law between 60% and 70% of the time. Similarly, policies supported by businesses and special-interest lobbies ended up being passed into law between 60% and 70% of the time. In contrast, policies supported by a majority of voters ended up being passed into law only about 30% of the time, and every single time one of those policies became law, it also had the support of either business lobbies, the rich, or both. According to the study, not a single policy supported by the majority of voters but opposed by the rich and the business community ended up being passed into law.

## Lie #9: Tax cuts for rich people will trickle down to regular people.

This one is so stupid that we almost didn't include it, but for those who are still confused, after decades of irrefutable proof, for the very last time, money does *not* trickle down from rich people to poor people. It trickles up from poor people to rich people when poor people buy things from the companies

rich people own. Every time you buy something, a little of your money trickles out of your bank account into my bank account in the form of a dividend or something like that from the company selling what you bought. Trotting out a disheveled Art Laffer every time someone wants to justify a tax cut does not change the direction of the trickle.

## Lie #10: Rich people should be trusted.

One last thing: whatever you do, please don't trust every rich person who claims they want to pay higher taxes. Some of them are lying.

Consider Eli Broad, a famous California philanthropist. Back in 2012, he stood with Jerry Brown, then governor of California, and publicly endorsed Brown's proposal to raise taxes on high-income earners, saying, "Those of us that are wealthy like myself should pay more."[33] Sounds great, right? Well, a *Los Angeles Times* investigation later revealed that Broad had actually secretly funneled $1 million through a series of organizations in Virginia and Arizona to a California advocacy group fighting *against* the tax increase that he publicly said he supported.[34] That's right, Broad wanted the public accolades that came with being a tax reformer, but his donation suggests he didn't really want the tax reforms he was publicly supporting.

No rich person, including any member of the Patriotic Millionaires, deserves to be taken at their word. Actions (and money) speak a lot louder than words, and that's how we should judge whether or not a rich person is actually on the right side of this fight. The next time a rich person claims they want to pay higher taxes; ask them how much money they are spending to accomplish that. Ask them how many lawmakers they have personally called to demand higher taxes. Ask them what percentage of their political funding goes to politicians committed to unrigging our economy. Ask them how many lobbyists they have hired to fight for higher taxes. They know how this system works. It they wanted higher taxes, they would act like it.

Is Eli Broad at it again? Just last year, Broad penned an op-ed for the *New York Times* titled "I'm in the 1%. Please, Raise My Taxes." Do you think he means it this time?

# Unrigging the Political Economy to Create a More Perfect Union (by Erica)

*You can fool all of the people some of the time and some of the people all of the time, but you cannot fool all of the people all of the time.*

—Abraham Lincoln

From the beginning, the American vision centered on justice and equality, but everyone knows that even out of the gate we often failed to live up to our ideals. We didn't even get the central premise of "one man, one vote" right at the beginning; we had to fight about it several more times along the way—heck, we are still fighting about it. In 1780, "one man" meant "one white property-owning man." After the Civil War, it meant "one man of any color," at least in theory. In 1920, women's suffrage became universal and "one man, one vote" became "one person, one vote," again, at least in theory. In 2020, it became "one person, one vote, unless the Russians interfere, and as long as the government doesn't shut down your polling place or lose your absentee ballot at the post office."

I like to think of our country's story as a never-ending negotiation toward a more perfect union for all of us. Those perpetual negotiations frequently involve the two most important and interrelated things in a capitalist democracy: power and money. These negotiations often come on the heels of incredible tension and social upheaval, and when they are successful, they lead to more power and more prosperity for more people.

Today, we are in the middle of one of those moments of renegotiation, and boy is this one a doozy. Money and power have been concentrated into the hands of too few for so long that things have gotten really unstable. Some say our country is crippled, that we've lost our greatness and will never recover, but I disagree. Maybe it's the cheerleader in me, but I believe we could look back years from now and see that all this tension, all these incredible challenges were paving the way for the greatest moment in American history. We can come out of these dark days stronger and build a future that will be remembered as the greatest period of prosperity, justice, and human dignity in all of human history.

Doing the right thing is always the right choice, even if it's hard. And frankly, taxing millionaires and billionaires is just not that hard. Let's see this moment for what it could be, an incredible opportunity to build a more perfect union. As we've said from the beginning, fixing things is actually not all that complicated; we just have to demand that our nationally elected leaders make the changes we need to see.

## Federal Leadership Is Essential

In the county's beginning, almost all U.S. policies were conducted by thirteen separate sovereign states. New York and Virginia were about as connected as Germany and Italy are today as members of the European Union. Then the federal government started creating some tariffs on imports, a tax on whiskey, and a few other things. That was about all the federal government did, until those whiskey taxes led to an armed rebellion in Pennsylvania that required military force to put down.[1] At the time of the Whiskey Rebellion, the federal government didn't have a military force, so it had to ask states to send their own troops voluntarily. That's how small the federal government was. It seems hard to imagine.

Since then, more and more power has moved from state governments into the hands of the federal government. As the country faced new challenges, we found that the federal government was best able to respond to the crises that affect us all. Here are a few examples:

- In the 1860s, in addition to defeating my traitorous fellow Southerners in the Civil War, after a U.S. banking crisis, the federal government began regulating banks—something that is now almost entirely a federal function.
- In 1910, the federal government passed the Mann Act, regulating interstate transportation for prostitution. That began the whole era of the federal government regulating everything from fees for shipping cargo

by train to forbidding racial segregation in bus stations.

- In 1913, in the face of another crisis (World War I) our nation made a decision to tax the very richest, implementing a national income tax on about 3% of the population. The Revenue Act of 1913 imposed a 1% tax on incomes above $3,000, with a top rate of 6% on incomes over $500,000.

- During the Great Depression, the federal government introduced laws for a minimum wage, Social Security, labor unions, financial-market regulation, rural electrification, and massive federal spending.

- In the 1940s and 1950s, the postwar federal government raised top income tax rates on wealthy individuals to over 90%, dramatically expanding the government's involvement in every area of the economy.

- In the 1960s, the federal government eliminated state and local laws that enforced racial segregation (the "Jim Crow" laws) in the Southern states.

- In the 1970s, we realized that our needs for clean air and clean water could not be addressed by states acting individually, and, again, we greatly expanded the responsibilities of the federal government.

Today, the country faces several intersecting crises, including recovering from a global pandemic and the economic shutdowns that followed. Millions of people are unemployed or underemployed, and many of the lost jobs are unlikely ever to return. A frightening number of people have been evicted from their homes, and families across the country face food shortages, despite the United States being the richest country on the planet. All of this, of course, is against the backdrop of global climate destabilization.

Some "states' rights" people feel that states and localities should handle things on their own, that the federal government should take a hands-off approach. In 2020, Senate Majority Leader Mitch McConnell even called for the country to allow the states to go bankrupt, rather than providing funds to bridge them through the crisis.[2] But whereas nearly every other developed country has benefited from a national response that has minimized the impact of the pandemic on their populations, abdication by America's federal government and a policy of "leaving things to the states" has done nothing but result in millions of sick people and hundreds of thousands of dead Americans, as the country lacks a unified and federally enforced response. Leaving to state and local governments the responsibility to steer the country out of the economic disaster will end just as poorly. As with other moments of national crisis, this one requires the leadership of the federal government. There simply is no other choice.

## The Federal Government Must Help the States

Neither the coronavirus nor the resulting economic disaster respects political borders or states' rights. Even if they did, states and localities don't have the resources to deal with either problem effectively. With unprecedented levels of unemployment, income tax receipts are down for state governments. And with much of the population quarantined and conserving their resources, sales taxes, revenues from parking meters, and other ways cities and states fund the things they need to pay for are also down. State and local budgets are suffering, and the important things that they spend money on—everything from education, transportation, and parks to pensions and health benefits for state and local employees—are already being cut to the bone.

With billions in budget shortfalls, states are going to have to either lay off thousands of schoolteachers, firefighters, social workers, and other public servants, or significantly raise taxes on their residents who still have money. Combine that revenue shortfall with increased health care and education costs (the two biggest expenses for most states and two of the most important ways a government can support its people), and you have a recipe for social disaster.

Clearly millionaires and billionaires should pay higher state and local taxes, but state and local politicians are at least as wary of raising taxes on their wealthiest citizens as their federal counterparts are. (State and local politicians have to raise money from rich people for their campaigns too, you know.) In New York, Governor Andrew Cuomo, a Democrat, refused to raise taxes on his state's billionaires during the pandemic and instead cut $400 million from the state's Medicaid payments to hospitals.[3]

Cuomo was worried enough about blowback from billionaires in his state that he chose to threaten the health care of thousands of people rather than ask a few dozen people to pay higher taxes. Cuomo seems to believe billionaires will actu- ally leave the state if their taxes go up. History has shown that that's mostly an idle threat. In fact, several years ago, when New York raised taxes on millionaires, the number of mil- lionaires in the state actually increased.[4] But you can't con- vince elected officials of that. And if they can't raise money from rich people, they either have to cut spending or raise money through sales taxes and fees and fines, which dispro- portionately hurt middle-class people and the poor.

That's why it's so important for the federal government to step in and help state and local governments to recover. It's a lot less likely that a rich person will move out of the United States and renounce their citizenship than it is that a wealthy Chicagoan will move to Kansas to avoid higher taxes.

## On Budgets: The Federal Government vs. the States

State and local governments have a fairly fixed amount of money to spend. Their budgets can be compared to a family budget, where a certain amount of money comes in through taxes or the sale of municipal bonds, and that's the amount of money they have to spend on things such as police, teachers, and social workers.

The federal government doesn't work like that. For a variety of reasons, in terms of federal spending, there is not a direct one-to-one correlation between money in and money out. (Among other things, the U.S. dollar is the world's reserve cur- rency, and we have the ability to increase the money supply.)

The specific details are not particularly important for our discussion, so let's just understand that the federal government's spending is not constrained by taxes in the same way that a state government is. That freedom means the federal government can and should be responsible for funding the things people need when state and local governments are unable to provide it. In economic terms, the U.S. government has the ability to spend countercyclically, meaning that when no one else has money, the federal government still does. Politicians like to complain about the deficit, but you will notice that they typically complain about the deficit only when it's the other party spending money. Lawmakers from former Vice President Cheney to Representative Ocasio-Cortez have declared that, as far as the federal government is concerned, "deficits don't matter."

The U.S. Congress is often divided on the question of whether the federal government should step in and help the states during a national crisis. There are two sides to the debate:

Door A: Let the states fend for themselves (supported by most Republicans). By their thinking, states such as New York and California are spending way too much money, and this is an opportunity to force them to scale back. We can bankrupt their education systems, cancel retirement pay for their teachers and other state employees, and finally teach the next generation of people that public service is a bad career choice.

Door B: Bridging state budgets is an entirely appropriate federal-government response to national disasters (supported by most Democrats). States are going to have huge revenue shortfalls in the wake of the COVID-19 crisis; the federal government should backstop those losses until states recover. Our nation overall is just as wealthy as it was before the pandemic, but that wealth is now much more concentrated in the hands of a small number of rich Americans. The federal government should make up for the loss of tax revenue from all the people whose lives were upended by the pandemic and continue to invest in our communities' education, security services, parks, and much more.

There is only one real choice if you care about this country. Just as in past crises, the federal government needs to step up and do what the states cannot. We cannot let them fend for themselves and cut vital programs that millions of Americans rely on.

By supporting state and local governments so they can continue to provide services that people rely on, and restructuring the tax code so that it distributes the tax responsibility more fairly and begins to mitigate inequality, the federal government can ensure that the next 250 years of American history are more stable and even more prosperous than the ones that came before.

## Progressives Need a Vision

There's an old story that when Michelangelo was asked how he created his famous *David* statue, he said that he just cut away all the bits of marble that weren't David. I'd like our country to have the *David* of tax codes; I think our citizens deserve it. We can start by cutting away all the bits of the new Republican tax code that aren't right. But we should do more than just that. Repealing the 2017 Tax Cuts and Jobs Act entirely appeals to a lot of progressives, but they need to face the fact that the tax code we had before Republicans totally rewrote it wasn't any good either. We need to sweep the pieces off the chessboard and just start over.

One problem with how the tax debate plays out is that right-wing conservatives have a big, overarching vision: lower taxes for rich people. The rest of the political establishment, in contrast, has a million small ideas for how to improve things, and a corresponding number of ideas about how to generate the money to pay for them. Sit in a meeting with lawmakers to discuss tax policy, and they will bring out a list of various tax ideas (they call them "pay fors") with an estimated amount of revenue that each tiny idea will generate. When they have a social program or a new project they want to fund, they pull out that list and add a few of those line items together until they get the amount of money they need to fund that specific priority (even though, as we have explained, in the federal government there is no one-to-one connection between taxes and spending).

This is no way to approach tax policy. A shopping list of societal benefits cross-referenced against a list of possible revenue items is not the best way to structure a tax system so that your political economy will generate better outcomes. Instead, we should back up a few steps and consider what we want our political economy to do holistically and then explore the ways we can reform the tax system within our political economy to ensure that happens.

Morris started the book with a warning to his fellow millionaires that went something like this:

- A society this unequal can't last.
- The pitchforks will come for you.
- They won't be pitchforks.

We know that the U.S. political economy as it is currently constructed is creating an increasingly unequal society where a very small number of people have an enormous amount of wealth, and millions have little or none. That inequality is creating divisions between our people, and providing an opening for cynical political operatives to exploit our fears and embolden our worst impulses, destabilizing the entire country and threatening our long-term peace and prosperity.

We need to restructure the economy so that it naturally creates more equitable outcomes. In the same way I deadhead my hydrangea bushes to encourage them to bloom, we can prune the growth of the fortunes of our billionaires to ensure that our whole society blossoms. There is significant evidence that inequality hurts economic growth, causes higher rates of health and social problems, and leads to lower overall happiness and life satisfaction. There is also a proven correlation between highly progressive tax systems (where the rich pay significantly more than we do here in the United States) and stable, happy societies. The 2018 UN World Happiness Report (yes, there is such a thing) reported that the happiest countries on earth were the countries that had the most progressive tax systems and economies that generated more equal returns.[5]

We need to eliminate our current tax system's enormous built-in advantages for wealthy people in order to have a political economy that will get us the society most Americans want.

## Unrigging the Economy Through the Tax Code

Here are six things we need to do to our tax code to start unrigging the economy:

### 1. Equalize Capital Gains and Ordinary Income Tax Rates for Incomes over $1 Million

The fact that rich investors who don't work for their money are allowed to pay a substantially lower tax rate than normal Americans who work for a living is the single most important thing to change about our current tax code.

We know that most people earning investment income are rich people, meaning this tax break ends up overwhelmingly benefiting rich people. We know that raising taxes on investors won't actually stop them from investing. We know that equalizing the capital gains tax rate and the income tax rate would decrease inequality. So let's do it!

It shouldn't matter whether you worked for your money or earned it from an investment. Actually, while we're at it, why not go even further? Let's consider raising the tax rate on capital gains even higher than the rate on ordinary income. If this country values hard work so much, why shouldn't the incomes of idle billionaires be taxed at a higher rate than

those of people who actually work for a living? There's a strong argument to be made that working Americans have a right to keep more of their income than have those who did nothing to earn theirs except for already being rich.

## 2. End the Bracket Racket:
## Create Lots of Brackets at Much Higher Rates

Most taxes paid by individuals, including income taxes and capital gains taxes, operate on a sliding scale where the more money you make, the higher the percentage of that money you pay in taxes. But instead of increasing gradually with each dollar you make, the tax rate "jumps" at certain amounts, creating the tax "brackets" that we're all familiar with. For example, currently, after deductions, the first $10,000 (roughly) of income is taxed at 10%, the next $30,000 (roughly) is taxed at 12%, with this process continuing at increasing rates until topping out at 37% for additional income over around $600,000. This system reflects our understanding of the marginal utility of money. We know that the more dollars you have, the less each dollar means to you, so we tax those additional dollars more.

We know that the wealthy can survive a higher income tax rate because the current top income tax rate is actually one of the lowest we've seen in modern American history.

At Davos in 2019, Dutch historian Rutger Bregman took on Michael Dell, the founder of the computer company Dell, after the billionaire said that he would not support a 70% tax rate and did not believe that rate would help the growth of the U.S. economy. When asked to explain his position, Dell said, "Name a country where that's worked—ever." Bregman had some information for Dell. "I'm a historian—the United States. That's where it has actually worked. In the 1950s, during Republican President Eisenhower, you know, the war veteran. The top marginal tax rate in the U.S. was 91 percent for people like Michael Dell. The top estate tax for people like Michael Dell was more than 70 percent . . . ['This is] not rocket science . . . We can talk for a very long time about all these stupid philanthropy schemes. We can invite Bono once more. But come on . . . We've got to be talking about taxes. Taxes, taxes, taxes. All the rest is bullshit in my opinion."[6]

Bregman knew what most Americans don't. Aside from a five-year stretch in the late 1980s and early 1990s, and the decade following the Bush tax cuts, the top marginal tax rate hasn't been below 38% since 1931. In fact, during the 1940s, 1950s, and 1960s—decades of explosive economic growth in the United States—the top marginal tax rate never went below 70%. For most of the 1950s, a decade seen by many as an economic golden age for the United States, the top marginal tax rate was 91%.[7] Our own history proves beyond a shadow of a doubt that higher top income tax rates are not the economic poison their opponents claim them to be—they're the antidote our society needs.

Keep in mind that a bipartisan majority of Americans support doubling our current top income tax rate: 59% of registered voters support raising the top income tax rate to 70%. But the breadth of the support, not just the total amount, is what's really surprising. While Republican lawmakers virtually unanimously oppose tax increases on the rich, a whopping

45% of Republican voters support a 70% top rate.[8] There's no reason—except the rich-people lobby—that there can't be additional higher brackets today.

### How It Would Work

Remember, raising the top rate does not mean that anyone paying the current top rate would suddenly pay the new top rate on all their income. Income would be taxed in exactly the same way it is now, at progressively higher levels as a person earns more and more—we just need to add more brackets and to tax each subsequent bracket substantially more.

Right now, a household earning over $612,000 a year pays a top rate of 37% on all of its members' income above $612,000, no matter how much more they make. While most really rich people earn their money through investment income instead of ordinary income, tens of thousands of people still earn millions of dollars a year in the form of a salary for work they do. Every single one of them can afford to pay more in taxes, and they should be required to pay a lot more. Should the top rate be, say, 70%, 80%, or 90%? We can debate that, but surely we can agree that it shouldn't be merely 37%.

While we tend to lump all rich people into the same category when talking about wealth and income in the United States, there are actually vast differences between different categories of wealthy people. Millions of people in the United States make a few hundred thousand dollars each year. Only about sixteen thousand make more than $10 million.[9] Differentiating these groups might feel like splitting hairs to someone who's working for the minimum wage, but when we're talking about effectively taxing the rich, we need to treat them differently.

There's a big difference between $650,000 a year and $65 million a year. Yes, someone earning $650,000 is still garden-variety rich and can definitely afford to pay more, but someone earning that amount probably still lives a relatively normal life, especially if she lives in an expensive city, such as New York. While $650,000 affords an extremely comfortable lifestyle, it's not enough to live like a king. She can send her kids to a very expensive school, go out to eat a lot, buy a nice house, and take a few luxurious vacations a year. But it's not enough money for her to do whatever she wants, whenever she wants. Someone earning tens of millions of dollars a year, on the other hand, is going to have a hard time finding enough ways to spend that money. Someone who takes in tens of millions from his investments could contribute a significant percentage through increased taxes without changing his lifestyle in the slightest. He might not even notice.

We shouldn't be treating these two kinds of rich people the same way. We need higher taxes on the rich (starting at $1 million in income), but we need even higher taxes on the super-rich, and even higher taxes than that on the uber-rich. The best system would have dozens of different brackets, each with a different rate—some north of 70%, 80%, or even 90%. This way, the super-rich would start to pay more than the garden-variety rich.

## The Tax-Bracket Racket

Contrary to what some may believe, moving up into a higher tax bracket doesn't mean you pay the higher rate on everything you've earned. You pay the higher rate only on whatever you earn inside that bracket. Your earnings below that bracket are taxed at a lower rate, and anything earned above the bracket is taxed at a higher rate.

Say you earn $40,000 a year after deductions, and you get a raise that brings you to $50,000 after deductions. You will pay 10% on the first $9,875; 12% on the amount from $9,876 to $40,125; and 22% on the remainder. So you don't pay the 22% on your entire income, only on the amount above $40,125.

That's what marginal rate actually means—it's the tax paid on the next dollar of income. If you're in the 35% bracket, you're not actually paying a total tax rate of 35%. You're going to pay much less than 35% of your total income in taxes, because different chunks of your income are still going to be taxed at the lower brackets of 10%, 12%, and so on. Only the portion between $207,351 and $518,400 will be taxed at 35%.

Rich people still pay the exact same tax rates as middle-class people do on the same amount of money; the rich just pay a higher rate on the money they make on top of that. Someone making $10 million a year only pays 22% on their 50,000th dollar, like everyone else. They just pay more on the $9,950,000 above that. So ignore all the billionaires whining about how high their tax rates are (we're talking about you, Steve Schwartzman!).

| Tax Rate | Single Taxpayers | Married Filing Jointly* | Married Filing Separately | Head of Household |
|---|---|---|---|---|
| 10% | Up to $9,875 | Up to $19,750 | Up to $9,875 | Up to $14,100 |
| 12% | $9,876 to $40,125 | $19,751 to $80,250 | $9,876 to $40,125 | $14,101 to $53,700 |
| 22% | $40,126 to $85,525 | $80,251 to $171,050 | $40,126 to $85,525 | $53,701 to $85,500 |
| 24% | $85,526 to $163,300 | $171,051 to $326,600 | $85,526 to $163,300 | $85,501 to $163,300 |
| 32% | $163,301 to $207,350 | $326,601 to $414,700 | $163,301 to $207,350 | $163,301 to $207,350 |
| 35% | $207,351 to $518,400 | $414,701 to $622,050 | $207,351 to $311,025 | $207,351 to $518,400 |
| 37% | $518,401 or more | $622,051 or more | $311,026 or more | $518,401 or more |

*Qualifying widow(er)s can use the joint tax rates

SOURCE: INTERNAL REVENUE SERVICE

## Historical Highest Marginal Tax Rates

| Year | Top Marginal Tax Rate | Year | Top Marginal Tax Rate | Year | Top Marginal Tax Rate | Year | Top Marginal Tax Rate |
|---|---|---|---|---|---|---|---|
| 1913 | 7.00% | 1941 | 81.10% | 1969 | 77.00% | 1997 | 39.60% |
| 1914 | 7.00% | 1942 | 88.00% | 1970 | 71.25% | 1998 | 39.60% |
| 1915 | 7.00% | 1943 | 88.00% | 1971 | 70.00% | 1999 | 39.60% |
| 1916 | 15.00% | 1944 | 94.00% | 1972 | 70.00% | 2000 | 39.60% |
| 1917 | 67.00% | 1945 | 94.00% | 1973 | 70.00% | 2001 | 39.10% |
| 1918 | 77.00% | 1946 | 86.45% | 1974 | 70.00% | 2002 | 38.60% |
| 1919 | 73.00% | 1947 | 86.45% | 1975 | 70.00% | 2003 | 35.00% |
| 1920 | 73.00% | 1948 | 82.13% | 1976 | 70.00% | 2004 | 35.00% |
| 1921 | 73.00% | 1949 | 82.13% | 1977 | 70.00% | 2005 | 35.00% |
| 1922 | 58.00% | 1950 | 84.36% | 1978 | 70.00% | 2006 | 35.00% |
| 1923 | 43.50% | 1951 | 91.00% | 1979 | 70.00% | 2007 | 35.00% |
| 1924 | 46.00% | 1952 | 92.00% | 1980 | 70.00% | 2008 | 35.00% |
| 1925 | 25.00% | 1953 | 92.00% | 1981 | 69.13% | 2009 | 35.00% |
| 1926 | 25.00% | 1954 | 91.00% | 1982 | 50.00% | 2010 | 35.00% |
| 1927 | 25.00% | 1955 | 91.00% | 1983 | 50.00% | 2011 | 35.00% |
| 1928 | 25.00% | 1956 | 91.00% | 1984 | 50.00% | 2012 | 35.00% |
| 1929 | 24.00% | 1957 | 91.00% | 1985 | 50.00% | 2013 | 39.60% |
| 1930 | 25.00% | 1958 | 91.00% | 1986 | 50.00% | 2014 | 39.60% |
| 1931 | 25.00% | 1959 | 91.00% | 1987 | 38.50% | 2015 | 39.60% |
| 1932 | 63.00% | 1960 | 91.00% | 1988 | 28.00% | 2016 | 39.60% |
| 1933 | 63.00% | 1961 | 91.00% | 1989 | 28.00% | 2017 | 39.60% |
| 1934 | 63.00% | 1962 | 91.00% | 1990 | 28.00% | 2018 | 37.00% |
| 1935 | 63.00% | 1963 | 91.00% | 1991 | 31.00% | 2019 | 37.00% |
| 1936 | 79.00% | 1964 | 77.00% | 1992 | 31.00% | 2020 | 37.00% |
| 1937 | 79.00% | 1965 | 70.00% | 1993 | 39.60% | | |
| 1938 | 79.00% | 1966 | 70.00% | 1994 | 39.60% | | |
| 1939 | 79.00% | 1967 | 70.00% | 1995 | 39.60% | | |
| 1940 | 81.10% | 1968 | 75.25% | 1996 | 39.60% | | |

**NOTES:** This table contains a number of simplifications and ignores a number of factors, such as the amount of income or types of income subject to the top tax rates, or the value of standard and itemized deductions.
**SOURCES:** IRS Revenue Procedures, various years; Eugene Steuerle, The Urban Institute; Joseph Pechman, Federal Tax Policy; Joint Committee on Taxation, Summary of Conference Agreement on the Jobs and Growth Tax Relief Reconciliation Act of 2003, JCX-54-03, May 22, 2003.

## 3. Tax the Rich!: Implement a Wealth Tax

Higher taxes on income, capital gains, and wealthy estates are all necessary parts of any comprehensive plan to tax the rich. They aim to stop the growth of inequality in America by limiting further accumulation of wealth by dynastic families. What they don't do, however, is undo the buildup of wealth that's already taken place.

It's certainly important to stop things from getting worse, but merely slowing or stopping the growth of inequality will fail to correct decades of wealth concentration. Tackling income inequality is not enough. Plugging a hole in the boat doesn't make a difference if the boat is already sinking.

Yes, we want to encourage economic growth. Yes, we want to raise enough money to finance the things we want to do. Yes, we want our tax code to disincentivize harmful behaviors and encourage good ones. We want our tax code to do all these things. But in the short term, we also need to use the tax code specifically to reduce inequality.

The top 1% of Americans *earn* about 20% of all income in the United States, but they *own* an even more disproportionate percentage of wealth in America. As a group, they own more than 40% of the nation's wealth, nearly twice as much as the bottom 90% of Americans combined. It gets even worse with the richest of the rich, the billionaires who have so much money they don't know what to do with it. Just the richest three people in the country own more wealth than the bottom half of all Americans combined—over 150 million people.

Most people know that economic inequality is bad, but they don't know it's *that* bad, because such extreme disparities are

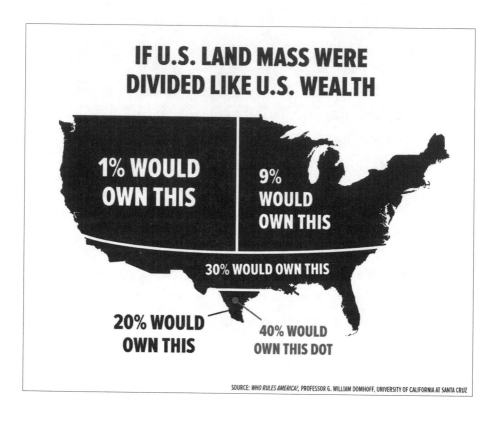

# IF U.S. LAND MASS WERE DIVIDED LIKE U.S. WEALTH

1% WOULD OWN THIS

9% WOULD OWN THIS

30% WOULD OWN THIS

20% WOULD OWN THIS

40% WOULD OWN THIS DOT

SOURCE: *WHO RULES AMERICA?*, PROFESSOR G. WILLIAM DOMHOFF, UNIVERSITY OF CALIFORNIA AT SANTA CRUZ

hard for the human mind to grasp. It doesn't feel real that a group small enough to fit into a single limousine could control more wealth than over 150 million people put together, but that's exactly the reality of today's America.

We certainly want to keep this problem from getting worse, but it's nowhere near enough to just freeze our current levels of inequality in place. We need to do more, and there's only one way to directly fix the fact that a very small number of people control a very large amount of the country's wealth—tax that wealth.

## The Basics

A wealth tax is a tax on the total value of everything a rich person owns. Add up the value of everything they own—from stocks to real estate to diamonds to boats to art to weird collections of ancient artifacts or rare beetles—subtract their debts, and take a percentage of that total every year.

Most people in America have some form of wealth, whether it's a car or a house or a few dollars in a bank account (although millions of Americans actually have more debt than wealth, giving them a negative net worth). But a wealth tax wouldn't tax everyone's wealth, just that of the absolute richest Americans. Senator Elizabeth Warren's wealth-tax proposal would tax wealth only above $50 million; and Senator Bernie Sanders's, only above $32 million. Any amount of wealth below that goes completely untaxed. This means both that only the ultrawealthy are affected by the wealth tax, and that a wealth tax can't tax anyone into poverty.

## Upping the Ante: The Warren and Sanders Wealth Taxes

Wealth taxes are a relatively new idea in the United States, only truly entering the mainstream political discussion when Senator Warren proposed a wealth tax during her presidential campaign in 2019. Her proposal of a 2% tax on wealth above $50 million and a 3% tax on wealth above $1 billion was groundbreaking, but it was soon followed by an even more aggressive version of a wealth tax proposed by Senator Bernie Sanders.

Warren and Sanders then got into a wealth-tax bidding war. The Sanders wealth tax expands upon the Warren plan to tax slightly lower levels of wealth, kicking in at $32 million, and to tax higher wealth at a higher rate, reaching up to 8% on fortunes worth over $10 billion. Warren then responded by raising her proposed tax rate on wealth over $1 billion from 3% to 6%.[10]

Each of these wealth taxes would raise immense amounts of revenue, with Warren's "Ultra-Millionaire Tax" projected to raise $2.75 trillion over a decade and Sanders's "Tax on Extreme Wealth" estimated to raise $4.35 trillion over a decade. That's a lot of money coming out of the pockets of billionaires, more than virtually any other tax proposal.

## Rich People Can't Stop Getting Richer

Once you're really rich, it's almost impossible to stop being rich. It's not unheard-of for people who own a few million dollars in assets to fall on hard times and drop down into the middle class. But once you become truly rich, with hundreds of millions or even billions of dollars in wealth, you'd have to

## Warren and Sanders Wealth Proposal Taxes

Here are the two proposals side-by-side, with examples of how much a super-rich person at a typical level would pay each year:[11]

### Warren's "Ultra-Millionaire Tax"

Rates

- 2% tax on wealth between $50 million and $1 billion
- 6% tax on wealth above $1 billion

Examples

- Someone worth $100,000 will pay $0
- Someone worth $1 million will pay $0
- Someone worth $100 million would pay $1 million per year ($0 on their first $50 million, and $1 million on their second $50 million)
- Someone worth $1 billion would pay $19 million per year
- Someone worth $10 billion would pay $199 million per year
- Jeff Bezos, worth approximately $125 billion at the beginning of 2020, would pay about $2.5 billion per year

## Sanders's "Tax on Extreme Wealth"

Rates

- 1% tax on wealth between $32 million and $50 million
- 2% tax on wealth between $50 million and $250 million
- 3% tax on wealth between $250 million and $500 million
- 4% tax on wealth between $500 million and $1 billion
- 5% tax on wealth between $1 billion and $2.5 billion
- 6% tax on wealth between $2.5 billion and $5 billion
- 7% tax on wealth between $5 billion and $10 billion
- 8% tax on wealth over $10 billion

Examples

- Someone worth $100,000 will pay $0
- Someone worth $1 million will pay $0
- Someone worth $100 million would pay about $1.2 million per year
- Someone worth $1 billion would pay about $32 million per year
- Someone worth $10 billion would pay about $607 million per year
- Jeff Bezos, worth approximately $125 billion at the beginning of 2020, would pay about $9.8 billion per year

be either extraordinarily unlucky or incredibly stupid ever to drop down into the ranks of the merely well-off.

Two competing principles govern how much wealth a person accumulates (or loses): how much is earned versus how much is spent. For average Americans, the amount earned every year through income hovers right around how much they spend each year, plus or minus a bit of savings or debt.

The same is true for many moderately wealthy people living off their investments. Assuming a 5% return on his investment, someone with a net worth of $1 million could live comfortably on $50,000 a year and never increase or decrease his wealth. Some people living off the return on their investments spend a little more than they earn each year, reducing their principal, or starting block of money. If someone with $1 million in wealth started spending $100,000 a year, she would end up $50,000 poorer at the end of each year. This would leave her earning a lower return the next year, because the return on her investment would be 5% of a lower amount than what she started with. If she kept this unsustainable spending up over time, she would end up running out of money.

The reverse is also true and is more common for the ultra-wealthy. When you spend less than you earn from your investments, you just keep getting richer. And thanks to the scale of many people's wealth, it's almost impossible for them to spend more than they're earning. A 5% return on $1 million is easy to spend every year, but a 5% return on $100 billion is an entirely different story.

## Compound Interest Is Unstoppable

Look at Bill Gates, the single most generous philanthropist in the world, who has promised to give away almost all his wealth to charity. Together with Warren Buffett, he launched the Giving Pledge, a campaign to get his fellow billionaires to pledge at least half their wealth to charity. He has donated more than $45 billion to various causes through the Bill & Melinda Gates Foundation, yet, as of 2020, he was still the second richest man in the world.[12] Even after all that giving, according to calculations from *Business Insider*, if Bill Gates suddenly stopped earning any return on his wealth and started spending $1 million per day, it would take him 285 years to spend it all. One million dollars to Bill Gates is the equivalent of $1 to the average American family.[13]

Despite the fact that he's given away tens of billions of dollars, Gates's wealth has actually more than doubled over the last ten years, rising from $54 billion in 2010, the year he signed the Giving Pledge, to over $110 billion in 2020. Bill Gates's net worth increased by $16 billion in 2019 alone.[14] That's almost impossible to spend, even for someone as charitable as Gates, so his wealth just keeps increasing. He can't stop getting richer.

Gates's fortune may be unique, but the trend isn't. Once you're that rich, it's almost impossible to spend enough to shrink your fortune. Lots of people can think of ways to spend $10 million, but it's much harder to spend $10 billion a year. You can buy whatever you want—cars, houses, planes, Rolexes, yachts—and they won't even make a dent.

This unstoppable accumulation of wealth is why we need a wealth tax. There's no other way to prevent the ultrarich from getting richer and richer and richer.

**You and Your Neighbors Probably
Already Pay a Wealth Tax**

Billionaires may complain about the idea of having to pay a percentage of their wealth in taxes every year, but wealth taxes are nothing new in America. Millions of American homeowners already pay a wealth tax every year—a property tax.

For middle-class Americans, much of their wealth is in their homes. This makes property taxes essentially a wealth tax for the average American. The average middle-class family has 61% of its wealth tied up in its home, while primary residences (the homes they actually live in) make up just 7.6% of the total wealth of the average family in the top 1%.[15] (Rich people own many other kinds of assets that go untaxed, from status symbols, such as jewelry, yachts, and artwork, to intangible assets, such as stocks, bonds, and other financial instruments.)

This means that even though richer people tend to live in more expensive homes, as a percentage of their total wealth and income, rich people end up paying significantly less in property taxes. Studies show that the richest 10% of income earners pay less than 2% of their incomes in property tax each year, while the poorest 10% pay almost 5% of their income in property tax each year, more than double what the rich pay.[16]

Expecting millionaires and billionaires to do exactly what most middle-class homeowners do—pay taxes on most of their wealth—is hardly too much to ask.

The top 1% holds just 7.6% of their wealth in their homes, while the average middle-class family has 61% of its wealth tied up in its home.

## 4. Stop Letting Investors Delay Tax Payments on Capital Gains: Mark-to-Market Taxation

Most Americans pay taxes every other week. Part of every paycheck is withheld, and then they file a tax return in April to complete any necessary reconciliation (payment or refund).

Unlike wages, which are taxed in real time, investment growth is taxed only at the point when the investment is sold. It doesn't matter how much more valuable an investment, such as a stock or a piece of property, gets over the course of a year; you don't have to pay a cent of taxes on it until you sell it.

So if Jeff Bezos owns $100 billion in Amazon stock at the beginning of the year, and over the next few months the value of that stock increases to $150 billion, even though he is (a lot) richer, until he cashes out, he doesn't owe anything to the government.

The U.S. government is missing out on trillions of dollars in taxes by letting rich people delay paying taxes until they sell their assets. This delay, combined with loopholes such as the stepped-up basis, is one of the biggest contributors to inequality in America. In order to tax the wealth of the richest people in America as it grows, we need to switch to a "mark-to-market system," where rich investors are taxed every single year on the increased value of the assets they own, giving them an annual tax bill just like everyone else.

The fact that rich people get to pick and choose when to sell their assets, and therefore when to pay taxes on the increased value of those assets, gives them a massive financial advantage over people who have to pay taxes on their paychecks every single year. Being able to decide when they pay their taxes means:

- Rich people get to time the sale of their assets to coincide with their other financial dealings, letting them line up their losses and gains to cancel out any taxes they would otherwise owe.
- Rich people can delay paying taxes for their entire lives and end up having their entire tax bill wiped out when they pass assets on to their heirs, thanks to the stepped-up basis.
- Rich people get even richer by being able to invest money they would otherwise pay in taxes, benefiting from the "time value" of money. Having $1 million today is much more valuable than having $1 million ten years from now, because if you have that money today, you can invest it and end up with significantly more money down the line. Similarly, paying taxes today is much more expensive than paying taxes ten years from now. If you can wait ten years to pay your taxes, you can invest the money you should be paying in taxes and end up making a significant amount of money from those investments, which you wouldn't have been able to make if you had to pay your taxes ten years ago.

## The Effect of Mark-to-Market

Compare the total net worth of Ms. Vera Riche, who has to pay taxes on the increased value of her assets every year under a mark-to-market system, and Mr. Richard Annew, who gets to pay his taxes only when he sells his assets.

Both start with $100 million, both have a 10% rate of return on their investments, and both pay a 20% capital gains tax rate. Everything but the timing of their taxes is exactly the same, but their totals after ten years end up dramatically different:

**Ms. Riche:**

*10% annual rate of return*

*20% tax on the increase in value every year*

Year 1: $100 million

Year 2: $108 million (plus 10% in increased value, minus 20% of that increased value deducted in taxes)

Year 3: $116.64 million

Year 4: $125.97 million

Year 5: $136.04 million

Year 6: $146.93 million

Year 7: $158.69 million

Year 8: $171.38 million

Year 9: $185.09 million

Year 10: $199.9 million

Subtotal: $199.9 million

**No additional tax**

Final Total: $199.9 million

**Mr. Annew:**

*10% annual rate of return*

*20% tax on the total increase in value when the total is sold after ten years*

Year 1: $100 million

Year 2: $110 million

Year 3: $121 million

Year 4: $133.1 million

Year 5: $146.4 million

Year 6: $161.05 million

Year 7: $177.16 million

Year 8: $194.87 million

Year 9: $214.36 million

Year 10: $235.8 million

Subtotal: $235.8 million

**20% tax on $135.8 million in increased value**

Final Total: $208.64 million

As you can see, Richard Annew, the millionaire who is able to defer payments, ends up with nearly $9 million extra. Now imagine thousands of millionaires and hundreds of billionaires going through this exact same process for multiple decades, and you can see how much of a difference the issue of timing makes when it comes to wealth accumulation.

## 5. Make Corporations Pay Taxes Where
## They *Really* Make Their Profits: End Profit Shifting

The corporate tax code is so complicated that a discussion of fixing it would take up an entire book. Let's first fix the single biggest problem—international profit shifting.

We need to change the rules of corporate taxation so that multinational corporations have to pay taxes in the countries where they actually earn their revenue—and are not allowed to get a tax deduction for money they transfer to other parts of their own corporations in foreign countries. This would force big corporations to play by the same rules as Main Street businesses. The current rules encourage investors to accumulate billions of dollars in the accounts of foreign corporations, even though almost all of that is still invested in the United States; it's just legally owned by a foreign corporation for tax purposes.

## 6. Make Sure They Actually Pay: Fund the IRS

No amount of tax reform will make a difference if rich people can just ignore the rules and not pay their taxes. It doesn't matter what rate they're technically supposed to pay if rich people can evade taxes with impunity. Enforcement is just as important as lawmaking.

Unfortunately, the government agency tasked with collecting taxes, the IRS, has been all but crippled by a decade-long effort to decrease the agency's auditing capabilities. Conservative anti-tax legislators have targeted the IRS for budget cuts since coming into power in the 2010 midterms. Since 2011, the IRS's enforcement budget has been cut by

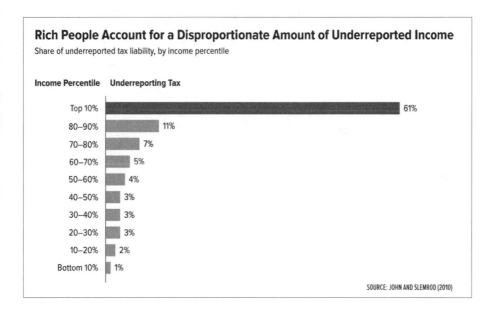

**Rich People Account for a Disproportionate Amount of Underreported Income**

Share of underreported tax liability, by income percentile

| Income Percentile | Underreporting Tax |
|---|---|
| Top 10% | 61% |
| 80–90% | 11% |
| 70–80% | 7% |
| 60–70% | 5% |
| 50–60% | 4% |
| 40–50% | 3% |
| 30–40% | 3% |
| 20–30% | 3% |
| 10–20% | 2% |
| Bottom 10% | 1% |

SOURCE: JOHN AND SLEMROD (2010)

nearly 25%.[17] Between 2010 and 2017, it lost 43% of its tax technicians and 44% of its revenue officers, leaving it with as many enforcement officers as it had in the 1950s, when the economy was one-seventh the size it is now.[18] That's simply not enough.

We need to increase funding for the IRS so we can hold tax cheats accountable. Our government's inability to catch tax evaders has been a problem for decades, but in its current state, the IRS is almost completely incapable of properly identifying and punishing tax evasion, particularly among wealthy households with much more complex finances. As a result, tax evasion in America has skyrocketed.

## The Tax Gap

Between 2011 and 2013, about 15% of all taxes owed to the government—nearly one-sixth of all federal taxes, totaling over $400 billion per year—ended up unpaid.[19] We don't have more recent data, but at that rate, around $600 billion would have gone missing from the federal coffers—our collective bank account—in 2018. That isn't just a colossal number, it also happens to be over 75% of the entire federal budget deficit in 2018. Some estimates put future losses even higher if nothing changes, with a cumulative total of 7.5 trillion missing dollars over the next decade.[20]

## Rich People Do It More

This isn't an issue that affects all income groups equally. There are obviously low-income households taking advantage of tax breaks they might not necessarily qualify for or failing to report income, but playing the system is a rich person's game. Most Americans work for a living, and taxes are taken out of every paycheck. They may not report every last dollar they earn on the side, but IRS data shows that the top 10% of income earners accounted for 61% of that $400 billion tax gap, while the bottom 90% accounted for way less than half the problem.

While average people are required to have money withheld from every paycheck, or to file quarterly if they have their own business, rich investors are supposed to decide for themselves how much to send in and send a check to the IRS every once in a while. Not surprisingly, this leads to a huge amount of abuse.

## Rich People Are More Likely to Get Away with It

Despite the fact that we know rich people are more likely to cheat on their taxes, the IRS doesn't audit rich people any more than it does poor people. The audit rates for poor Americans and the top 1% are extremely similar. Why? Because the IRS doesn't have the resources to go after more rich people.

There's no way an understaffed agency can compete with the armies of accountants and tax lawyers fielded each year by wealthy individuals and corporations. It takes skilled, specially trained auditors to properly unravel the layers of complexity in the tax return of a billionaire or corporation, and there simply aren't enough to get the job done. Even those who do have this expertise are now more likely than ever to leave their increasingly low-paying and overworked jobs at the IRS to work for the other side, using their knowledge of the tax code to help the rich avoid instead of pay taxes.

"It's not enough to write 'Megabucks' on your return, Mr. Clacton. You're supposed to tell us how many."

Without this expertise, all the IRS can do is pursue the simplest, most clear-cut cases, which in many instances means a disproportionate focus on poor and middle-income Americans. It's much easier to match up someone's wages to their W2 than it is for the IRS to verify that wealthy businesspeople are properly calculating and reporting their taxable income.

Because of this lack of resources, audits on millionaires have plummeted. From 2011 to 2019, the proportion of millionaires who were audited dropped from 12% to just 3%,[21] while fewer than 1% of all corporations are now audited each year.[22] Annual audit rates for large corporations—those with assets over $10 million—also fell from 17.8% in 2012 to just 7.9% in 2017.[23]

Instead of targeting millionaires, in recent years the IRS has particularly targeted taxpayers who make use of the Earned Income Tax Credit, which is available only to low-income households. These people tend to earn less than $20,000 a year, yet they are being audited at rates similar to people making $500,000 to $1 million per year. This is clearly absurd. When poor Americans are being targeted for audits while billionaires are getting away with massive tax fraud, a serious realignment of agency priorities is clearly necessary. But that's not going to be possible without giving the IRS the resources necessary to go after the top-level cheats.

**It's a Strategy, Not an Accident**
For most people, the IRS's inability to audit the rich properly might seem like a problem, but to those who fought to cut the agency's budget, it's a wild success. Neutering the IRS isn't a

sad side effect of otherwise necessary budget cuts; it was the goal all along.

Most cuts to the federal budget are made in the name of "fiscal responsibility," or cutting the deficit, but that's clearly not the case here. Cutting funding for the IRS is the opposite of fiscal responsibility. When the government spends more money on tax enforcement, it actually makes back many times more in increased revenue—it's an excellent investment. Yet between 2010 and 2018, the IRS budget was cut by around $1.5 billion (adjusted for inflation). According to a ProPublica report, those cuts ended up costing the U.S. government at least $18 billion per year, if not tens of billions of dollars more.[24] Experts estimate that investing an additional $100 billion in IRS enforcement would raise about $1.1 trillion over ten years.[25]

If every dollar you spend on enforcement returns around ten times that amount, it would seem to make sense to spend more money on enforcement. And when the gap between what is owed in taxes and what is actually paid is around three-quarters of the entire federal budget deficit, it would make sense to spend more money on making sure those taxes are paid. What is actually going on here?

It's a vicious cycle. The wealthy make campaign donations to politicians. They then petition the politicians for favorable policy changes—tax loopholes, rates that benefit rich investors, defunding the IRS—and threaten to withhold future campaign contributions if they don't get what they want. The politicians comply. The wealthy donors take advantage of all the policies that favor them and then some. The defunded

IRS fails to enforce. And the rich get richer. This allows them to make even more campaign donations, and . . . you get the picture.

That's why the unrigging ideas in this chapter are so important. They will disrupt this terrible cycle and pave the way to a more stable and equitable society. Now let's talk about how we're going to get it done.

# Here's How We Do It

*Taxes are the dues that we pay for the privileges of membership in an organized society.*
　　　　　　　　　　　　—President Franklin D. Roosevelt

We know what we need to do to fix our tax code. The only thing we don't know is whether or not we can build the political will to get it done.

Unfortunately, rich people in America have a huge amount of political power, and regular people don't. That's just a fact. When rich people want the government to do something (or not do something, when it comes to taxing them), they tend to get their way. When the interests of the rich are stacked up against the well-being of everyone else in the country, the rich tend to win more often than not. But it doesn't have to be that way.

There are a lot of obstacles in our path, but we have one thing on our side that can beat every card the oligarchs will play—the people. Even though our political system is deeply flawed and infected with the corrupting influence of billions of dollars of dark money, at the end of the day, it's still a democracy. Yes, the system is stacked against the people in the fight for a fair tax code. But nothing the millionaires and billionaires do can stand in the way of an educated, engaged, and united electorate. And the American people are already united around taxing the rich—pretty much everyone already agrees with us—so now we just need to unleash that energy onto our lawmakers.

## Polling

In poll after poll, the American people say that they want to raise taxes on the rich. This is one of the few issues that cross party lines, with Democrats, independents, and Republicans all agreeing that rich people and corporations don't pay enough in taxes.

In an era of bitterly divided partisanship, it's rare to find something that the right and the left both agree on. But polling shows that a majority of Americans from all walks of life believe both that our economy has a problem and that we need to tax the rich to fix it. For decades, politicians have claimed their pro-corporate and pro-campaign-donor positions are "moderate," but they're actually wildly out of step with the will of the people; the truth is that taxing the rich is one of the most popular *bipartisan* positions in the United States. The politicians who want to keep rigging the economy for their campaign donors are the real radicals.

## Everybody Wants to Tax the Rich

A September 2017 Morning Consult/Politico poll showed that 61% of respondents believe that the wealthy pay too little in taxes, while only 14% believe that they pay too much.[1]

A collection of polls in 2019 showed that 76% of registered voters want the wealthiest Americans to pay more in taxes, while 65% of registered voters support increasing taxes on families earning over $1 million a year and 70% support increasing taxes on those earning over $10 million per year.[2] In another poll that year, 48% thought that low-income people pay too much in taxes, while 62% think that the rich pay too little.[3] A November 2019 Hart Research poll also showed that 80% of voters say that making sure the wealthy pay their fair share is important.[4] A 2020 Reuters/Ipsos poll showed that nearly two-thirds of respondents, including 77% of Democrats and 53% of Republicans, agreed with the idea that "the very rich should contribute an extra share of their total wealth each year to support public programs."[5]

Even the bolder "tax the rich" proposals have broad support among the American people.

Fifty-nine percent of registered voters support raising the top marginal income tax rate to 70%, with 45% of Republican voters, 71% of Democrats, and 60% of independents in favor of it.[6] Senator Elizabeth Warren's wealth tax has been shown to be supported by 86% of Democrats, 69% of independents, and 65% of Republicans.[7] Even a majority of millionaires support the wealth tax, with a 2019 CNBC poll showing that 60% of millionaires would support a Warren-style wealth tax.[8] On

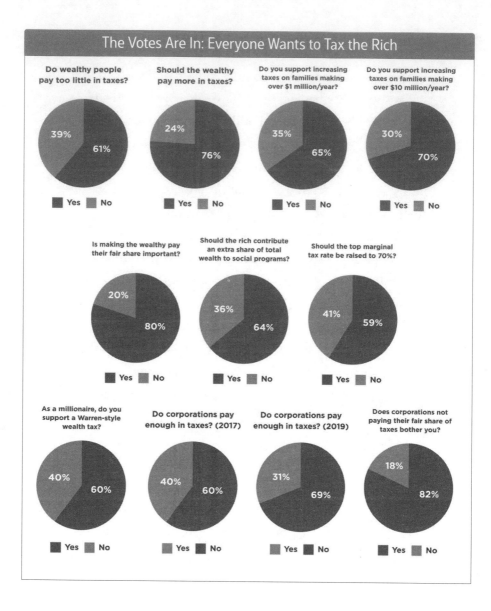

### The Votes Are In: Everyone Wants to Tax the Rich

**Do wealthy people pay too little in taxes?**
39% No · 61% Yes
■ Yes ■ No

**Should the wealthy pay more in taxes?**
24% No · 76% Yes
■ Yes ■ No

**Do you support increasing taxes on families making over $1 million/year?**
35% No · 65% Yes
■ Yes ■ No

**Do you support increasing taxes on families making over $10 million/year?**
30% No · 70% Yes
■ Yes ■ No

**Is making the wealthy pay their fair share important?**
20% No · 80% Yes
■ Yes ■ No

**Should the rich contribute an extra share of total wealth to social programs?**
36% No · 64% Yes
■ Yes ■ No

**Should the top marginal tax rate be raised to 70%?**
41% No · 59% Yes
■ Yes ■ No

**As a millionaire, do you support a Warren-style wealth tax?**
40% No · 60% Yes
■ Yes ■ No

**Do corporations pay enough in taxes? (2017)**
40% Yes · 60% No
■ Yes ■ No

**Do corporations pay enough in taxes? (2019)**
31% Yes · 69% No
■ Yes ■ No

**Does corporations not paying their fair share of taxes bother you?**
18% No · 82% Yes
■ Yes ■ No

the corporate side, in 2017, a Morning Consult/Politico poll showed that 60% of registered voters think that corporations don't pay enough in taxes.[9] And this poll was conducted when the corporate tax rate was still 35%—it has since dropped to just 21%.

Recent Gallup polling shows 69% of Americans now say corporations pay too little in taxes.[10] March 2019 polling by the Pew Research Center found 82% of Americans are at least bothered "some" or "a lot" by corporations not paying their fair share.[11]

## The President + the Gang of Four

Getting a bill turned into a law doesn't just take building popular support or getting a broad consensus among lawmakers—it requires power. In Congress, power is concentrated in a small number of members—essentially four key people—in leadership positions. They make the final decisions about which bills live or die.

Unrigging the tax code requires getting the President and the Gang of Four—the Speaker of the House, the Chair of the House Ways and Means Committee, the Senate Majority Leader, and the Chair of the Senate Committee on Finance—on our side. That congressional quartet holds absolute power over the fate of the U.S. tax code. And we have exactly two tools at our disposal to win their support for change:

1. Political leverage: You're not going to convince congressional leaders to change their position on an issue such

as taxation through debate, but you may convince them to act out of political necessity. They have a lot of power, but at the end of the day, they still need the cooperation of the rest of their caucus to govern, and they need their constituents to vote for them. Build up enough support for legislation among either of those two groups, and the leadership will be pressured to bend.

2. Replacement: Sometimes Congress members just won't change their minds on an issue, no matter how much their colleagues and constituents try to change them. If, say, a committee chair and the Senate Majority Leader have made it clear they'll never pass any bills that raise taxes on the rich, the only option is to remove them from their positions of power and replace them with more reasonable leaders.

## Vote the Bastards Out

Ultimately, winning this fight is going to take changing the makeup of Congress. Some members of the House and Senate may be willing to change their minds, and some may be susceptible to real, sustained pressure from their constituents. But take it from people who have spent a lot of time over the last few years trying to convince members of Congress to raise taxes on the rich—many of our elected representatives are lost causes. They have no intention of ever raising taxes on rich people, and no amount of political pressure is going to change their minds.

Who are these members of Congress? Well, for starters, basically every Republican. We're not going to bullshit you and act as if both parties are equally bad in order to make ourselves look unbiased. They're not equally bad. When it comes to taxes and rich people, the Republican party as currently constructed is a lost cause. It exists as a political extension of corporate and wealthy America that uses wedge social issues to build up popular support for politicians who then make unpopular economic policies.

Look at what happened when Trump came into power with a Republican-controlled Senate and House. The first and only major piece of legislation they passed with full control of the federal government was the Tax Cuts and Jobs Act, a $2 trillion giveaway to the rich. They've shown us who they are, and until they start behaving differently, it's safe to assume that any Republican candidate for anything is terrible on taxes.

But don't just assume that Democrats are all great on taxes. There are lots of Democrats in Congress who have just as little interest in taxing the rich as their Republican colleagues have. They may *talk* more about economic fairness, but at the end of the day, there are dozens of Democrats in Congress who have absolutely no interest in unrigging the economy and taxing the rich.

What should we do if we can't change politicians' minds? Simple: we vote them out and replace them with lawmakers who recognize the responsibility their offices hold to help create a more stable and equitable society.

## Not All Litmus Tests Are Bad

In some corners of Washington, it's become "smart" to be dismissive of political litmus tests. And it's true that using a candidate's position on one key issue to decide whether to support them is not always a good idea. If a candidate agrees with you on most things, the thinking goes, then you should support them. For some things, this approach makes sense. But some things are too fundamental to consider compromising on.

If a lawmaker isn't with us on making the country more equitable, they're against us. The tax code is one of the single most important tools the government has to structure the political economy and mitigate the inequality that is tearing our nation apart. Choosing not to reform the tax code is an open endorsement of the disastrous status quo. No one who is fine with the way our political economy currently works should be allowed to represent us in a position of power, and it's our duty as voters to ensure that the people we send to Washington understand what's at stake.

Ask every candidate running for office in your town or state or district whether or not they support raising taxes on the rich. They should provide a yes-or-no answer. If they can't clearly say, without a shadow of a doubt, that they are 100% in favor of raising taxes on the rich, then they don't deserve your vote.

## A Fairer America

If we want to see where our current tax code will take us, we need only look at where we've been. Pre-eighteenth-century England suffered a permanent, entitled upper class that held a monopoly on wealth, and a permanent underclass trapped in poverty and servitude. Moving up economically was virtually impossible, and those at the top considered themselves superior to everyone else, with the "right" to treat those born without silver spoons in their mouths as if they were not human.

Most people who came willingly to America in the last four hundred years, came in order to build better lives for themselves and their children, in a country that had made a founding commitment to fairness and justice (however unrealized it then was or still is). We have always aspired to being a land of opportunity. Nothing threatens that aspiration more than the current structure of the political economy.

Money and power. Power and money. It's a story as old as civilization itself. We wrote this book in the hope that our fellow citizens—those who are millionaires and those who are not, people in both parties and no party at all—will read it and be inspired to think about taxes in a new way, and then act.

The Other Millionaires will be difficult to beat. They honestly believe that they *deserve* special treatment, and they will fight like hell to ensure they get it. But now that you've read this book, you will have the tools you need to beat them.

When they call themselves job creators and insist that the economy will collapse if (God forbid!) they are asked to pay a single penny more in taxes, you will know that they are lying. Millionaires put their pants on one leg at a time, just like everyone else. Consumer demand is the only real job creator. And nothing is going to collapse if they lose their built-in advantage in the tax code (apart from an overinflated ego or two).

America's political economy, led by the tax system at its heart, has the power to set the country on a better, fairer, and more sustainable course, and it's up to all of us to ensure that we get there.

# Dedications

**From Erica:**
Dedicated to my husband, Gene, and our daughter, Ilsa Ruth. You made my life.

**From Morris:**
Dedicated to

- My wife Barbara, who is at my side through every adventure.
- My parents, who instilled into me the belief that I could do anything.
- My sons, Joshua and Adrian, of whom I am so proud.
- Mi nuera Donaira, que ha traído mucha felicidad a mi familia.
- And my granddaughter, Zagora, who embodies the future of my family and whose generation embodies the future of our nation.

# Acknowledgments

**From Morris and Erica:**

With very special thanks and a huge debt of gratitude to Sam Quigley and Rene Felt, without whom this book would not have been possible. We would like to thank Diane Wachtell, Rachel Vega-DeCesario, Emily Albarillo, and the team at The New Press, as well as the Bookbright Media team, who helped us move our ideas from our brains to our keyboards and then transformed them into this beautiful book in your hands.

# Notes

## A Note from Morris Pearl

1. The Economist/YouGov Poll, April 8–11, 2016, d25d2506sfb94s.cloudfront.net/cumulus_uploads/document/lmrt74ordg/econTabReport.pdf.

2. Christopher Ingraham, "There Are More Guns Than People in the United States, According to a New Study of Global Firearm Ownership," *Washington Post*, June 19, 2018.

## A Note from Erica Payne

1. Katherine Clarke, "Billionaire Ken Griffin Buys America's Most Expensive Home for $238 Million," *Wall Street Journal*, January 23, 2019.

2. Courtney Comstock, "Steve Schwarzman on Tax Increases: 'It's like When Hitler Invaded Poland,'" *Business Insider*, August 16, 2010. Following the well-trod path of other rich people who suffer backlash when their offensive sensibilities are brought to the attention of the public, Schwartzman did eventually apologize.

3. Graham Flanigan, "CEOs and Business Leaders Are 4 Times More Likely to Be Psychopaths Than the Average Person," *Business Insider*, October 26, 2016.

4. "Attorney General James Files Nation's Most Comprehensive Suit Against Opioid Distributors and Manufacturers," *Office of the New York State Attorney General*, March 28, 2019, ag.ny.gov/press-release/2019/attorney-general-james-files-nations-most-comprehensive-suit-against-opioid.

5. Melissa D. Berry, "The Sackler Family, the Opioid Crisis & Liability for Corporate Wrongdoing," Legal Executive Institute, May 21, 2019, www.legalexecutiveinstitute.com/sackler-family-opioid-crisis.

6. "Nearly One in Three People Know Someone Addicted to Opioids," *American Psychiatric Association*, www.psychiatry.org/newsroom/news-releases/nearly-one-in-three-people-know-someone-addicted-to-opioids-more-than-half-of-millennials-believe-it-is-easy-to-get-illegal-opioids.

7. Dylan Matthews, "Meet the Folk Hero of Davos: The Writer Who Told the Rich to Stop Dodging Taxes," Vox, January 30, 2019, www.vox.com/future-perfect/2019/1/30/18203911/davos-rutger-bregman-historian-taxes-philanthropy.

## 1: What Exactly Is "Rich"?

1. Arielle Mitropolous, "Biden to ABC's David Muir on Raising Taxes: 'No New Taxes' for Anyone Making Less Than $400,000," ABC News, August 23, 2020.

2. Chuck Collins, "Billionaire Bonanza: The Forbes 400 and the Rest of Us," Institute for Policy Studies, November 2017, inequality.org/wp-content /uploads/2017/11/BILLIONAIRE-BONANZA-2017-Embargoed.pdf.

3. "The Forbes 400: The Definitive Ranking of the Wealthiest Americans," *Forbes*, October 2, 2019.

4. Juliana Menasce Horowitz, Ruth Igielnik, and Rakesh Kochhar, "Trends in Income and Wealth Inequality," Pew Research Center, January 2020, www .pewsocialtrends.org/2020/01/09/trends-in-income-and-wealth-inequality.

## 2: WTF Is the "Economy," and Why Do the People Who Wrote This Book Keep Calling It the "Political Economy"?

1. *Encyclopaedia Britannica Online*, Academic ed., s.v. "Economic System," accessed October 5, 2020, www.britannica.com/topic/economic-system.

2. Investopedia, "Economy," accessed October 5, 2020, www.investopedia .com/terms/e/economy.asp.

3. Board of Governors of the Federal Reserve System, "Report on the Economic Wellbeing of US Households in 2017," May 2018, 2, www.federalreserve .gov/publications/files/2017-report-economic-well-being-us-households -201805.pdf.

4. Gabriel Zucman, "Global Wealth Inequality," National Bureau of Economic Research, January 2019.

5. National Institute on Drug Abuse, "Effective Treatments for Opioid Addiction," June 4, 2020, www.drugabuse.gov/publications/effective -treatments-opioid-addiction.

6. Laura Santhanam, "American Life Expectancy Has Dropped Again. Here's Why," PBS, November 29, 2018.

## 3: How to Rig an Economy

1. Scott Eastman, "How Many Taxpayers Itemize Under Current Law?," Tax Foundation, September 12, 2019, taxfoundation.org/standard-deduction -itemized-deductions-current-law-2019.

2. Leonard E. Burman, "Capital Gains Cuts Won't Cure the Covid-19 Economy," Tax Policy Center, May 11, 2020, www.taxpolicycenter.org/taxvox /capital-gains-cuts-wont-cure-covid-19-economy.

3. Chuck Marr, Samantha Jacoby, and Kathleen Bryant, "Substantial Income of Wealthy Households Escapes Annual Taxation or Enjoys Special Tax Breaks," Center on Budget and Policy Priorities, November 13, 2019, www.cbpp.org/research/federal-tax/substantial-income-of-wealthy-households-escapes-annual-taxation-or-enjoys.

4. Burman, "Capital Gains Cuts."

5. Sergei Klebnikov, "Jeff Bezos Gets $6.4 Billion Richer as Amazon Stock Hits a New Record High," *Forbes*, April 14, 2020.

## 4: Tax Tricks

1. Mikaela Lefrak, "Why This Billionaire Is Spending a Fortune on Washington's Monuments," NPR, February 13, 2020.

2. Alec Macgillis, "The Billionaires' Loophole," *New Yorker*, March 7, 2016.

3. Drew Armstrong, "The Medieval Geniuses Who Invented Carried Interest and the Modern Barbarians Who Want to Tax It," Foundation for Economic Education, March 20, 2017, fee.org/articles/the-medieval-geniuses-who-invented-carried-interest-and-the-modern-barbarians-who-want-to-tax-it.

4. Isabel V. Sawhill and Edward Rodriguez, "Wealth, Inheritance, and Social Mobility," The Brookings Institution, January 30, 2015, www.brookings.edu/blog/social-mobility-memos/2015/01/30/wealth-inheritance-and-social-mobility.

5. Internal Revenue Service, "What's New—Estate and Gift Tax," www.irs.gov/businesses/small-businesses-self-employed/whats-new-estate-and-gift-tax.

6. Rep. Kristi Noem, "My Voice: Estate Tax Was a Burden to My Family," *Argus Leader*, December 16, 2017, www.argusleader.com/story/opinion/2017/12/16/my-voice-estate-tax-burden-my-family/957097001.

7. Chuck Collins, "She's the Poster Child for Estate Tax Repeal, but Her Sad Family Saga Doesn't Add Up," *USA Today*, December 11, 2017.

8. Chloe Cho, "The Myth That the Estate Tax Threatens Small Farms," Center on Budget and Policy Priorities, April 4, 2017, www.cbpp.org/blog/the-myth-that-the-estate-tax-threatens-small-farms.

9. Robert Pozen, "This Is the Tax Break America's 1% Will Cling To—Even After Death," *MarketWatch*, December 14, 2019, www.marketwatch.com/story/this-is-the-tax-break-americas-1-will-cling-to-even-after-death-2019-12-11.

10. Naomi Jagoda, "Bennet, Romney Offer Compromise Proposal amid Year-End Tax Talks," *The Hill*, December 16, 2019.

11. Zachary R. Mider, "Accidental Tax Break Saves Wealthiest Americans $100 Billion," *Bloomberg*, December 17, 2013, www.bloomberg.com/news

/articles/2013-12-17/accidental-tax-break-saves-wealthiest-americans-100
-billion?sref=I6K1T2KU.

12. Robert Frank, "'Only Morons Pay the Estate Tax,' Says White House's Gary Cohn," CNBC, August 29, 2017.

13. Jesse Drucker and Eric Lipton, "How a Trump Tax Break to Help Poor Communities Became a Windfall for the Rich," *New York Times*, August 31, 2019.

14. Aaron Krupkin and Adam Looney, "9 Facts About Pass-Through Businesses," Brookings Institution, May 15, 2017, www.brookings.edu/research/9 -facts-about-pass-through-businesses.

15. Center on Budget and Policy Priorities, "Pass-Through Deduction Benefits Wealthiest, Loses Needed Revenue, and Encourages Tax Avoidance," March 27, 2019, www.cbpp.org/research/federal-tax/pass-through-deduction -benefits-wealthiest-loses-needed-revenue-and-encourages.

16. Matthew Smith, Danny Yagan, Owen M. Zidar, and Eric Zwick, "Capitalists in the Twenty-First Century," The National Bureau of Economic Research, June 2019, www.nber.org/papers/w25442.

17. Alicia Parlapiano, "How the 'Small-Business Tax Cut' Would Also Be a Tax Cut for the Wealthy," *New York Times*, December 20, 2017.

## 5: The Double Irish Dutch Sandwich
## and Other Corporate Tax Machinations

1. Toby Sterling, "Google to End 'Double Irish, Dutch Sandwich' Tax Scheme," Reuters, December 31, 2019.

2. Steve Denning, "The Origin of 'The World's Dumbest Idea': Milton Friedman," *Forbes*, June 26, 2013.

3. Institute on Taxation and Economic Policy, "Corporate Tax Avoidance in the First Year of the Trump Tax Law," December 16, 2019, itep.org/corporate -tax-avoidance-in-the-first-year-of-the-trump-tax-law.

4. Institute on Taxation and Economic Policy, "Corporate Tax Avoidance in the First Year of the Trump Tax Law," December 16, 2019, itep.org/corporate -tax-avoidance-in-the-first-year-of-the-trump-tax-law.

5. Michael Sainato, "'He Pulled the Wool Over Our Eyes': Workers Blame Trump for Moving Jobs Overseas," *The Guardian*, July 10, 2019.

6. "GE's $200-mn Manufacturing Unit in Pune," *Hindustan Times*, September 26, 2011, www.hindustantimes.com/business/ge-s-200-mn-manufact uring-unit-in-pune/story-SiMpr1h5hV71fUUicIKeiK.html.

7. Kaja Whitehouse, "Zuckerberg Tops CEO List with $3.3B Pay," *New York Post*, December 20, 2013, nypost.com/2013/12/20/zuckerberg-tops-ceo-list -with-3-3b-pay.

8. Brandon Ballenger, "Why Facebook Gets a $429 Million Tax Refund," *Yahoo! Finance*, February 18, 2013.

9. Matthew Knittel, "Corporate Response to Accelerated Depreciation: Bonus Depreciation for Tax Years 2002–2004," Office of Tax Analysis: US Department of Treasury, May 2007, www.treasury.gov/resource-center/tax-policy/tax-analysis/Documents/WP-98.pdf.

10. "The Tax Break-Down: Accelerated Depreciation," Committee for a Responsible Federal Budget, September 20, 2013. www.crfb.org/blogs/tax-break-down-accelerated-depreciation.

11. Amazon 2018 Annual Report, 2018, s2.q4cdn.com/299287126/files/doc_financials/annual/2018-Annual-Report.pdf.

## 6: On Lies and Liars

1. Andrea Elliott, "Invisible Child," *New York Times*, December 9, 2013.

2. Michael Ricciardi, "A Rigged Game of Monopoly Reveals How Feeling Wealthy Changes Our Behavior," *Planet Save*, December 23, 2013, planetsave.com/2013/12/23/a-rigged-game-of-monopoly-reveals-how-feeling-wealthy-changes-our-behavior-ted-video.

3. Matthew J. Belvedere, "AT&T CEO Says a Corporate Tax Cut Would Mean Thousands More Jobs for 'Hard Hat' Workers," CNBC, May 4, 2017.

4. Matthew Gardner, "GOP Leaders Tout Corporate Tax Cuts at Boeing and AT&T, Companies that Already Have Single-Digit Tax Rates," ITEP, August 23 2017, itep.org/gop-leaders-tout-corporate-tax-cuts-at-boeing-and-att-companies-that-already-have-single-digit-tax-rates.

5. Sarah Anderson, "Report: Corporate Tax Cuts Boost CEO Pay, Not Jobs," Institute of Policy Studies, August 30, 2017, ips-dc.org/report-corporate-tax-cuts-boost-ceo-pay-not-jobs.

6. Anderson, "Report: Corporate Tax Cuts Boost CEO Pay, Not Jobs."

7. ExecPay.org, "Randall Stephenson," www.execpay.org/executive/randall-stephenson-6930.

8. Drew FitzGerald, "AT&T Chief's Pay Jumped to $32 Million After Hedge Fund Battle," *Wall Street Journal*, March 12, 2020.

9. Anderson, "Report: Corporate Tax Cuts Boost CEO Pay, Not Jobs."

10. Emily Stewart, "What Is Private Equity, and Why Is It Killing Everything You Love?" *Vox*, January 6, 2020, www.vox.com/the-goods/2020/1/6/21024740/private-equity-taylor-swift-toys-r-us-elizabeth-warren.

11. DowneastDem, "How Private Equity Destroyed Toys 'R' Us," *Daily Kos*, September 30, 2017, www.dailykos.com/stories/2017/9/30/1702985/-How-Private-Equity-Destroyed-Toys-R-Us.

12. Toys "R" Us, Inc. United States Securities and Exchange Commission Form 10-K, Fiscal Year Ending January 29, 2005, getfilings.com/00001193125 -05-090701.html.

13. "Trio of Toys 'R' Us Stores Closing in Colo.," *Denver Business Journal*, January 9, 2006, www.bizjournals.com/denver/stories/2006/01/09/daily12.ht ml.

14. Jim Baker, Maggie Corser, and Eli Vitulli, "Private Equity: How Wall Street Firms Are Pillaging American Retail," *Popular Democracy*, July 2019, populardemocracy.org/sites/default/files/Pirate%20Equity%20How%20 Wall%20Street%20Firms%20are%20Pillaging%20American%20Retail%20 July%202019%20FINAL%20UPDATED%207-23-2019.pdf.

15. Chavie Lieber, "Why Bankrupt Toys R Us Might Not Be Dead After All," *Vox*, October 3, 2018, www.vox.com/the-goods/2018/10/3/17932344/toys-r-us -liquidation-coming-back.

16. Chris Isidore, Jackie Wattles, and Parija Kavilanz, "Toys 'R' Us Will Close or Sell All US Stores," *CNN Business*, March 15, 2018, money.cnn.com /2018/03/14/news/companies/toys-r-us-closing-stores/index.html.

17. Abha Bhattarai, "How Can They Walk Away with Millions and Leave Workers with Zero?: Toys R Us Workers Say They Deserve Severance," *Washington Post*, June 1, 2018.

18. Erin Palmer, "Business Leaders Hit Capitol Hill to Fight for Minimum Wage Increase," *Business Administration Information*, March 27, 2014, www .businessadministrationinformation.com/news/business-leaders-hit-capitol -hill-to-fight-for-minimum-wage-increase.

19. Rex Nutting, "Amazon Is Going to Kill More American Jobs Than China Did," *MarketWatch*, March 15, 2017, www.marketwatch.com/story/amazon-is -going-to-kill-more-american-jobs-than-china-did-2017-01-19.

20. Brad Tuttle, "Jeff Bezos Is Now Making an Astonishing $230,000 Every Minute," *Business Insider*, March 9, 2018, www.businessinsider.com /jeff-bezos-is-now-making-an-astonishing-230000-every-minute-2018 -3#:~:text=Amazon%20CEO%20Jeff%20Bezos%20is,%24231%2C000%20 per%20minute%20in%202018.

21. Megan Henney, "How Much Do Billionaires Donate to Charity?" *Fox Business*, November 26, 2019, www.foxbusiness.com/money/how-much-do -billionaires-donate-to-charity.

22. Robert Frank, "How Much Would a Wealth Tax Really Raise? Dueling Economists Reflect New Split in Democratic Party," CNBC, July 10, 2019, www.cnbc.com/2019/07/10/dueling-economists-debate-how-much-a-wealth -tax-would-raise.html.

23. Isabel V. Sawhill and Edward Rodrigue, "Wealth, Inheritance, and Social Mobility," Brookings Institution, January 30, 2015, www.brookings.edu/blog /social-mobility-memos/2015/01/30/wealth-inheritance-and-social-mobility.

24. Tim Roemer, "Why Do Congressmen Spend Only Half Their Time Serving Us?," *Newsweek*, July 29, 2015, www.newsweek.com/why-do-congressmen-spend-only-half-their-time-serving-us-357995.

25. Alexandra Bruell, "Political Ad Spending Will Approach $10 Billion in 2020, New Forecast Predicts," *Wall Street Journal*, June 4, 2019.

26. Dave Gilson, "It's Not the 1 Percent Controlling Politics. It's the 0.01 Percent," *MotherJones*, April 23, 2015, www.motherjones.com/kevin-drum/2015/04/one-percent-campaign-giving.

27. Reid Wilson, "How Citizens United Altered America's Political Landscape," *The Hill*, January 21, 2020, thehill.com/homenews/campaign/479270-how-citizens-united-altered-americas-political-landscape.

28. Department of Justice, US Attorney's Office, "Congressman Christopher Collins Pleads Guilty to Insider Trading Scheme and Lying to Federal Law Enforcement Agents," October 1, 2019, www.justice.gov/usao-sdny/pr/congressman-christopher-collins-pleads-guilty-insider-trading-scheme-and-lying-federal.

29. Cristina Marcos, "GOP Lawmakers: Donors Are Pushing Me to Get Tax Reform Done," *The Hill*, November 7, 2017.

30. Ned Resnikoff, "Princeton Scholar: Poor and Middle Class Have No Say in Government Policy," MSNBC, August 16, 2012, www.princeton.edu/~mgilens/Gilens%20homepage%20materials/MSNBC%20review%20of%20A&I/13317619-princeton-scholar-poor-and-middle-class-have-no-say-in-government-policy.

31. Jacqueline Thomsen, "Charles Koch Donated $500k to Ryan Days After GOP Tax Plan Passed," *The Hill*, January 21, 2018.

32. Kayla Kitson, "The Koch Brothers' Best Investment," *American Prospect*, June 28, 2018, prospect.org/power/koch-brothers-best-investment.

33. David Zahniser, "Philanthropist Eli Broad Endorses Brown's Call to Raise Taxes," *Los Angeles Times*, January 18, 2012.

34. Anthony York, "List Unmasks Secret Donors to California's Initiative Campaigns," *Los Angeles Times*, October 24, 2013.

## 7: Unrigging the Political Economy to Create a More Perfect Union

1. Peter Kotowski, "Whiskey Rebellion," Washington Library Center for Digital History, www.mountvernon.org/library/digitalhistory/digital-encyclopedia/article/whiskey-rebellion.

2. John Wagner, "McConnell Takes Flak After Suggesting Bankruptcy for States Rather Than Bailouts," *Washington Post*, April 23, 2020.

3. Denis Slattery, "No Major Medicaid Cost Shift to NYC in Budget, but

Cuomo Restructuring Includes Hospital Cuts," *New York Daily News*, April 3, 2020.

4. Joseph Spector and Sean Lahman, "Number of NY Millionaires Rose 63 Percent Since 2009," *Democrat and Chronicle*, March 17, 2017, www .democratandchronicle.com/story/news/politics/albany/2017/03/17/number -ny-millionaires-rose-63-since-2009/99311558.

5. United Nations, "UN World Happiness Report 2018," March 14, 2018, worldhappiness.report/ed/2018.

6. Morgan Gstalter, "Historian Accuses Billionaires at Davos of Not Paying Their Fair Share in Taxes," *The Hill*, January 30, 2019.

7. Tax Policy Center, "Historical Highest Marginal Income Tax Rates." www.taxpolicycenter.org/statistics/historical-highest-marginal-income-tax -rates.

8. Matthew Sheffield, "Poll: A Majority of Americans Support Raising the Top Tax Rate to 70 Percent," *The Hill*, January 15, 2019.

9. Daniel B. Kline, "Who Would Pay a 70% Tax Rate on Income Over $10 Million?," *Motley Fool*, January 9, 2019, www.fool.com/investing/2019/01 /09/who-would-pay-a-70-tax-rate-on-income-over-10-mill.aspx.

10. Jacob Pramuk, "'Billionaires Should Not Exist': Bernie Sanders Tries to Outdo Elizabeth Warren with Tougher Wealth Tax Proposal," CNBC, September 24, 2019.

11. Huaqun Li and Karl Smith, "Analysis of Sen. Warren and Sen. Sanders' Wealth Tax Plans," Tax Foundation, January 27, 2020, taxfoundation.org /wealth-tax.

12. Kelsey Piper, "Bill Gates Is Committed to Giving Away His Fortune—But He Keeps Getting Richer," *Vox*, April 23, 2019, www.vox.com/future-perfect /2018/12/11/18129580/gates-donations-charity-billionaire-philanthropy.

13. Katie Warren, "11 Mind-Blowing Facts That Show Just How Wealthy Bill Gates Really Is," *Business Insider*, May 14, 2019, www.businessinsider.com /how-rich-is-bill-gates-net-worth-mind-blowing-facts-2019-5.

14. Tom Metcalf and Erik Schatzker, "How Bill Gates Has Boosted His Net Worth by $16 Billion This Year," *Fortune*, September 17, 2019.

15. Nick Routley, "How the Composition of Wealth Differs, from the Middle Class to the Top 1%," *Visual Capitalist*, May 8, 2019, www.visualcapitalist.com /composition-of-wealth.

16. Meg Wiehe, Aidan Davis, Carl Davis, Matt Gardner, Lisa Christensen Gee, and Dylan Grundman, "Who Pays? A Distributional Analysis of the Tax System in All 50 States," Institute on Taxation and Economic Policy, October 2018, itep.org/wp-content/uploads/whopays-ITEP-2018.pdf.

17. Paul Kiel and Jesse Eisenger, "How the IRS Was Gutted," *ProPublica*, December 11, 2018, www.propublica.org/article/how-the-irs-was-gutted.

18. Sara Estep, "Not Enough Cops on the Beat: IRS Cuts Have Benefited

Wealthy Tax Cheats," Center for American Progress, April 11, 2019, www
.americanprogress.org/issues/economy/news/2019/04/11/468594/not-enough
-cops-beat-irs-cuts-benefited-wealthy-tax-cheats.

19. William G. Gale and Aaron Krupkin, "How Big Is the Problem of Tax
Evasion?," Brookings Institution, April 9, 2019, www.brookings.edu/blog/up
-front/2019/04/09/how-big-is-the-problem-of-tax-evasion.

20. Robert Frank, "Tax Avoidance by the Rich Could Top $5 Trillion in Next
Decade," CNBC, November 19, 2019.

21. Alain Sherter, "Fear a Tax Audit by IRS? Don't—The Odds Are with You,"
CBS News, March 8, 2019.

22. Jim Buttonow, "How Likely Is an IRS Audit for a Client?," *Financial Planning*, January 29, 2019, www.financial-planning.com/news/what-are-a-clients
-chances-of-an-irs-audit.

23. Emily Horton, "Underfunded IRS Continues to Audit Less," Center on
Budget and Policy Priorities, April 18, 2018, www.cbpp.org/blog/underfunded
-irs-continues-to-audit-less.

24. Kiel and Eisenger, "How the IRS Was Gutted."

25. Frank, "Tax Avoidance."

## 8: Here's How We Do It

1. Bernie Becker, "North Dakota, Here We Come," *Politico*, September 6, 2017,
www.politico.com/tipsheets/morning-tax/2017/09/06/north-dakota-here
-we-come-222131.

2. "National Tracking Poll #190202," *Morning Consult*, February 2,
2019, morningconsult.com/wp-content/uploads/2019/02/190202_crosstabs
_POLITICO_RVs_v1_AP.pdf.

3. "Taxes," Gallup, 2019, news.gallup.com/poll/1714/Taxes.aspx.

4. Guy Molyneux and Geoff Garin, "Americans' Tax Priority: Make the
Wealthy Pay Their Fair Share," Hart Research, November 7, 2019, surtax.org
/wp-content/uploads/2019/11/Memo-Hart-ATF-Taxes-Winning-Issue-Nov
-7-Presser-E-12697.pdf.

5. Howard Schneider and Chris Kahn, "Majority of Americans Favor
Wealth Tax on Very Rich," Reuters/Ipsos, January 10, 2020, www.reuters.com
/article/us-usa-election-inequality-poll/majority-of-americans-favor-wealth
-tax-on-very-rich-reuters-ipsos-poll-idUSKBN1Z9141.

6. "Poll: A Majority of Americans Support Raising the Top Tax Rate to 70 Percent," *The Hill*, January 15, 2019, thehill.com/hilltv/what-americas-thinking
/425422-a-majority-of-americans-support-raising-the-top-tax-rate-to-70.

7. Laura Wronski, "New York Times | Survey Monkey Poll: November
2019," Survey Monkey, November 11, 2019, www.surveymonkey.com/curiosity
/nyt-november-2019-cci.

8. Robert Frank, "Most Millionaires Support a Tax on Wealth above $50 Million, CNBC Survey Says," CNBC, June 12, 2019, www.cnbc.com/2019 /06/12/most-millionaires-support-tax-on-wealth-above-50-million-cnbc -survey.html.

9. Becker, "North Dakota, Here We Come."

10. Megan Brenan, "Tax Day Update: Americans Still Not Seeing Tax Cut Benefit," Gallup, April 12, 2019, news.gallup.com/poll/248681/tax-day-update -americans-not-seeing-tax-cut-benefit.aspx.

11. Pew Research Center, "Growing Partisan Divide over Fairness of the Nation's Tax System," April 4, 2019, www.people-press.org/2019/04/04 /growing-partisan-divide-over-fairness-of-the-nations-tax-system.

# About the Authors

**Morris Pearl**, a former managing director of BlackRock, is chair of the Patriotic Millionaires, a group of hundreds of high-net-worth Americans committed to making all Americans better off by building a more prosperous, stable, and inclusive nation, and ensuring that millionaires, billionaires, and corporations pay their fair share of taxes. He lives in New York City.

**Erica Payne** is the group's founder and president. A graduate of the Wharton School and the author of *The Practical Progressive*, she lives in Washington, DC.

# Publishing in the Public Interest

Thank you for reading this book published by The New Press. The New Press is a nonprofit, public interest publisher. New Press books and authors play a crucial role in sparking conversations about the key political and social issues of our day.

We hope you enjoyed this book and that you will stay in touch with The New Press. Here are a few ways to stay up to date with our books, events, and the issues we cover:

- Sign up at www.thenewpress.com/subscribe to receive updates on New Press authors and issues and to be notified about local events
- Like us on Facebook: www.facebook.com/newpress books
- Follow us on Twitter: www.twitter.com/thenewpress
- Follow us on Instagram: www.instagram.com/thenew press

Please consider buying New Press books for yourself; for friends and family; or to donate to schools, libraries, community centers, prison libraries, and other organizations involved with the issues our authors write about.

The New Press is a 501(c)(3) nonprofit organization. You can also support our work with a tax-deductible gift by visiting www.thenewpress.com/donate.